BY JEN MANN

People I Want to Punch in the Throat

Spending the Holidays with People I Want to
Punch in the Throat

Spending the Holidays with People I Want to Punch in the Throat

Spending the Holidays with People I Want to Punch in the Throat

Yuletide Yahoos, Ho-Ho-Humblebraggers, and Other Seasonal Scourges

Jen Mann

BALLANTINE BOOKS

NEW YORK

Published in the United States by Ballantine Books,
an imprint of Random House, a division of
Penguin Random House LLC, New York.

BALLANTINE and the HOUSE colophon are registered trademarks
of Penguin Random House LLC.

Photos from the personal collection of the author.

LIBRARY OF CONGRESS CATALOGING-IN-PUBLICATION DATA
Mann, Jen.
Spending the holidays with people I want to punch in the throat : yuletide
yahoos, ho-ho-humblebraggers, and other seasonal scourges / Jen Mann.
pages cm
ISBN 978-0-345-54999-0 (paperback)—ISBN 978-0-8041-7629-3 (eBook)
1. Christmas—Humor. I. Title.
PN6231.C36M36 2014
818'.602—dc23   2015025901

Snowflake pattern from istockphoto/Aleksandar Veljasevic

Printed in the United States of America on acid-free paper

randomhousebooks.com

9 8 7 6 5 4 3 2 1

This book is dedicated to the Hubs, Gomer, Adolpha, and my family—thank you for supporting me, inspiring me, believing in me, and allowing me to write about all of you.

This book is also dedicated to my readers—thank you for finding me and "getting" me.

Contents

SECTION TWO:
Making My Own Christmas Memories (Note: They Still Suck)

Author's Note

So you think you might be one of the characters in this book? Oh, please. You're far too boring to be in this book. You really do think highly of yourself, don't you? All of the names and circumstances in this book have been changed to protect the good, the bad, and the ugly. These are my stories and this is how I remember them. You might remember them differently. If you do, then you should go write your own book.

Introduction

This book will make the perfect white-elephant gift at your office holiday party. It will no doubt help you to find "your people" instantly. You will quickly know if Gypsy at reception has a sense of humor and whether or not you should invite her to join your wine club—I mean book club. If Fritz in accounting doesn't start laughing as soon as he sees the cover, then you know you should find a new place to work. But a word of caution: don't give your boss this book. Most bosses don't have a sense of humor, and it could be a bad move for you and your career. I can't have that on my conscience.

I wrote this book because I come from a long line of Christmas overachievers on my mother's side of the family. Her mother grew up on a farm in Canada with her six sisters. On Christmas Eve their father would put them to bed and tell them to stay put no matter what they heard. Then he'd go out to the barn, hitch up the horses to their sled, and drive all over the front yard of their farmhouse ringing sleigh bells. The little girls—who slept two and three to a bed—would quiver and giggle with excitement, believing that Santa had arrived.

In the morning they'd find sled tracks in the snow and half-eaten carrots strewn around the yard, and they'd believe in the magic for another year.

I'm convinced this Yuletide gene skipped my generation. Well, maybe not my whole generation—I have cousins who would argue with me on this point. But it skipped me, at least.

To help you better navigate the essays in this book, here's a quick who's who of some of the people you'll encounter. I'm Jen. I'm a sarcastic, kind of bitchy, funny, sometimes offensive, middle-aged, tired, married mother of two who tends to say out loud (with as many profanities as possible) what everyone else is thinking. I have two kids: Gomer (age ten at the writing of this book) and Adolpha (age eight). Before you have a hissy fit and sit down to write me a nasty letter about my children's horrible names, just stop. *Of course* those aren't their real names.

Their real names are worse, but I can't take the ridicule, so I just made up what I consider to be horrific names for my blog, People I Want to Punch in the Throat, and my books. Are you still writing that letter? Why? Because your kid's name is Gomer and you take offense that I just called it "horrific"? Ugh. Actually, you know what? Go ahead, I don't care. Write away. As long as you bought this book, you can bitch at me about anything you'd like.

I'm married to the Hubs. His name isn't important; you can call him the Hubs, too. Everyone does. He's a cheap bastard who can be a tad antisocial, but he treats me like gold, so he's my lobster. Oh yeah, he's Chinese and I'm Caucasian. Sometimes that information is good to know when you're reading these essays.

I was raised by a professional Overachieving Mom (OAM) and my father, her enabler. When I was growing up, my dad encouraged my mom to stay home and follow her dreams of investing their retirement nest egg in her version of porn: crazy-ass expensive Santa Claus figurines and nativity sets. Hundreds of them. No joke. She has Santas that are baking cookies, decorating Christmas trees, and coming down chimneys, as well as one jogging in boxer shorts. She has nativity sets made of glass, pewter, and wood. One of her favorites is a six-pack of empty beer cans that were painted to resemble the holy family and the three wise men. She even has a few Santas holding mangers. (I just blew your mind, didn't I? Yeah, because nothing says "Jesus is the reason for the season" like a Santa Claus figurine holding the baby Jesus.)

I have a younger brother I call C.B.—not his real name, either. (From here on out, you can just assume that every name you read in this book besides Jen has been changed. Jenni, sadly, is real.) He has an important real job in the real world and is a tad concerned that his boss might read this book. (As if his boss reads anything but *Robb Report* and *Yachting Magazine*!) Anyway, C.B. would like to remain as anonymous as possible just in case he decides to run for president someday or join a country club. He's married to Ida and they have two kids, Sherman and Violet.

So, getting back to the theme of this book, when I was growing up my mother made sure that holidays were always an Event (with a capital *E*) for me and my brother. She made our stockings, she decorated her trees (yes, that's plural, as in numerous trees) with themes like "Snowmen" and "Angels" and "Good Tree—Don't Touch" and "Crappy Family Tree Where I Hang All of the Homemade Ornaments the Kids Made" (I don't think she really calls her tree that, but that's what I call it when I'm helping her decorate it). She went to extreme measures to keep us believing. When I was nine or ten, I was starting to doubt the existence of Santa, so she hired some old guy with a red suit and a beard to stop by our house on a Sunday afternoon a week or so before Christmas. I'm sure she thought I'd buy his routine and continue to believe for another year or so. I remember that day distinctly. I was in my room looking out my window when I saw him pull up in front of our house in a beat-up red pickup truck. He checked his teeth in the mirror on the back side of his sun visor, picked his nose, smoothed his beard, and spit his gum out the truck window. He threw on his red hat and sauntered up to our front door. Any ounce of belief I'd had prior to that went out my bedroom window. There was no way this guy was legit. I don't know what my mom spent, but she should have demanded a refund.

It's not my family's fault, however, that I ended up so grumpy during the holidays. It's not like I've had to share a turkey with a drunk uncle or had a teenage cousin who said, "Please pass the potatoes, I'm pregnant" during a Yuletide meal. So while we might not be fully dysfunctional, we are a bit ... odd, as my mother likes to say. The holidays have always been a sort of a balancing act for us. On one side I have my mom's family. My mom and her sister, my aunt Ruby, make holiday decorating a competitive Olympic sport, where second place is first place for losers. Their brothers do things like send me the same gift every year because they can't remember what they gave me last year and give their wives cash to go shopping at the day-after-Christmas sales so they can get "exactly what they want." On my dad's side of the family I have Jewish relatives who decorate Hanukkah bushes and wish me a merry Christmas while stuffing my hands with gelt. I wish them a happy Hanukkah and pocket that dough.

With all of this bah-humbuggery, it's no real surprise that I ended up writing a book titled *Spending the Holidays with People I Want to Punch in the Throat*. It's not that I hate the holidays; I just despise the nonsense that goes along with them. I don't know what it is, but as soon as "Jingle Bells" starts playing on the radio (on November 1!), the Overachieving Moms start raising that homemade-candy-cane bar and it drives me crazy. I decided years ago that I was done trying to get over that bar. I don't pose my family in matchy-matchy outfits for a picture that no one except my mother will keep. Although I look like someone who likes cookies, I rarely attend a cookie exchange unless I know there will be alcohol. No one in my neighborhood is jealous of my Christmas lights display. No one lines up for miles to see my pitiful, barely twinkling lights thrown haphazardly over a couple of bushes. And I am always the mom who on December 2 stops remembering to move her Elf on the Shelf. No, I am quite happy ducking under that candy-cane bar with my instant hot cocoa and store-bought cookies. I like buying my presents online so I don't have to fight the crowds of holiday shoppers mainlining Christmas cheer and pumpkin-spiced lattes.

It used to be just Christmas that brought out this madness, but now it's creeping into other holidays as well. My mother decorates for Halloween, Easter, and the Fourth of July. My kids' classmates get bicycles from the Easter Bunny and throw half-birthday parties. And lately I'm hearing about some madness called a Switch Witch. She's another damn doll. This one takes all of your Halloween candy and leaves presents instead. Oh great. Just what I need. Another damn magical doll to remind me what a terrible mother I am.

It pains my mother greatly that I can barely tolerate the holidays, but she is thrilled to know that I am raising a future Christmas fanatic. My daughter, Adolpha, is like the daughter my mother never had. She has not one but three miniature Christmas trees in her room. Yes, you read that right. I wrote "trees," but hold on. I also wrote "miniature," so that makes it better. Except that they're each three feet tall. That's nine feet of trees in one room! It's kind of ridiculous, I know. Her trees sport themes like "Ooh La La, Paris" (pronounced "Paree," with pink poodles and silver Eiffel Towers), "Fancy Disco Balls" (you know, jewel-toned mirrored ball ornaments), and "Pink Snowflakes" (pretty self-explanatory). Every year I make my mother go through her hundreds of boxes of Christmas decor and purge at least ten items. Those ten items never end up in the trash or the donate pile; they always end up in Adolpha's room. She's like a Christmas pack rat. She sees something shiny, and she grabs it and squirrels it away under her bed or in the back of her closet. Over the years she has amassed enough stuff for a fourth tree whose only theme could be described as "Grandma's Cast-offs." My guess is, this year my mom will buy that fourth tree for her.

And I will let her. I might not enjoy all of the decorating and the exhausting schedules that people try to keep during the holidays, but Adolpha loves it. She's taking my mom's old decorations because she's the sentimental one. It takes so little time for me to get her trees out of the attic so she can decorate them with weird little felt mice in Santa hats or bears dressed like baby Jesus (yeah, besides Santa holding baby Jesus, my mom has a weird Christmas animal fetish thing going on). Adolpha is the family historian who will carry on the tradition of being an overachiever, and someday when I'm old and my parents are gone, I will visit Adolpha's house so I can remember.

Family Christmas photo 1986. Between the awful perm and the braces, it's amazing I had anything to smile about that year. No wonder my eyes are closed.

Spending the Holidays with People I Want to Punch in the Throat

10 THINGS I HATE ABOUT THE HOLIDAYS

I am sure if you pressed me, I could come up with a few things I like about the holidays, but this book isn't about what I like, now is it? Maybe that will be my next book. Ha! As if I could come up with that many pleasant things to say. Nah, I think I'll just stick to what I do best: punch lists.

Pumpkin-flavor everything. Pumpkin lattes start showing up in August, and then it just snowballs from there. I don't even like pumpkin in a pie, but no one wants to eat a pumpkin Popsicle.

Douchey dads who can't take their kids trick-or-treating without pulling a wagon of beer behind them. What is the deal? This is a pretty easy job and isn't very stressful. It takes a couple of hours to walk through the neighborhood, wave to the person at the door, and yell something like, "Anything good for me? *Yuk, yuk, yuk.*" Why do these dads feel the need to be hammered before they take on this job?

Shopping for gifts. I am not a thoughtful shopper. I'd love to give everyone a gift card to Target or Amazon and call it a day, but I've been told that's not really fun for people to open on Christmas morning. (Side note to my family: *I* think those are great gifts. Feel free to give me a gift card anytime you'd like.) Another problem is that everyone on my list already has everything they want and/or need, or I can't afford what they really want. For instance, the Hubs would like a new watch. Easy, right? Not so much. A Timex will not do for this man. He would like a two-thousand-dollar watch. Gomer would like a four-hundred-dollar Lego set, and Adolpha would appreciate half of the American Girl store. It's not just them. I've got my eye on an eight-hundred-dollar Herman Miller Aeron chair that I'm pretty sure would help me write a Pulitzer Prize–winning novel.

The events. The holidays are a time to gather with friends and family. Everyone hosts a cookie exchange or a Christmas party or a special dinner, not to mention the winter parties and the concerts at school you've got to find time for. It's funny, no one wants to hang out with me in June, but I'm booked from Thanksgiving to New Year's. No wonder people are depressed when the holidays are over! You're the belle of the ball all winter, but as soon as Valentine's Day comes no one wants to see your face again until Halloween.

The food. I have a love/hate relationship with holiday fare. It's so damn good, but it's also so damn bad. I convince myself that eating twenty chocolate-covered peanut butter balls is perfectly fine because I only get them "once a year." What other time of the year is it acceptable to sit down to a five-course meal and then eat the leftovers a couple of hours later with a piece of pie on the side? Every party has delicious food to stuff your face with. I'm sure there's a veggie tray in the mix somewhere, but I never see it. Plus, who wants a celery stalk when you can have chocolate at every holiday celebration from Halloween to Easter?

Anyone who gets offended if they aren't wished the proper holiday. "Merry Christmas," "Happy Hanukkah," "Joyous Kwanzaa," "Feliz Navidad," "Wonderful Winter Solstice." Whatever. At least someone took the time out of their day to say "Have a great holiday season" to you. There is no need to be a dick. You don't have to get your hackles up because you don't celebrate whatever holiday they're wishing you. Just say thank you, asshole.

Christmas music *everywhere.* I'm certain there are more than fifteen Christmas songs, but it sure doesn't feel like it when you hear the same damn ones everywhere you go. It also annoys me that stores start playing them in October. I guess I kind of understand playing Christmas music in retail stores, because it's a subliminal message to get people motivated to start their holiday shopping, but there are some places it really doesn't make sense. For instance, I do not need, nor do I want, to hear "Away in a Manger" when I'm pumping gas. I have to fill up my tank regardless of the season. It's not like listening to holiday music will make me say, "Ooh, it's Christmastime, I think

I need to upgrade to premium gas today. A little holiday splurge!"

Bell ringers who hound you. Hey, dipshit, I gave when I went into the store. Don't look for me to give on the way out, too.

Kids home on winter break. This is another love/hate one. Each year, come December I have visions of the four of us decorating the house, baking cookies, and making homemade gifts for our friends, our family, and the neighbors. Then I wake up on the first day of winter break and the kids are fighting with each other and whining for television and food. We try to decorate the tree, but their "help" just creates more fighting and stress, because they're moving so slowly and I just want it to be *done already*. We never bake, because none of us can make a cookie that anyone would want to eat. Adolpha and I can work in the craft room for hours, but Gomer always finishes his projects in fifteen minutes and then complains he's bored. And the Hubs refuses to join in on any of the memory making, choosing instead to take a nap.

Moving the Elf on the Shelf. Obviously.

Christmas Memories I'd Like to Forget

BEFORE *TODDLERS & TIARAS* THERE WAS ME

I am four years older than my brother, C.B., so you would think that I would remember a Christmas or two without him, but I don't. I'm sitting here thinking of all the Christmas memories I can come up with, and they *all* involve him.

It's weird, because I'm pretty sure that even though he's the favorite child, we celebrated before he came along. Didn't we? I'm sure we did. Although I can't find any pictures. Whenever C.B. and I complain that there aren't many photos from different periods of our childhood, our parents tell us the camera was "broken" then. I guess the camera was broken at every Christmas until C.B. was born. How convenient.

Wait! I do have a memory of a Christmas before C.B. Well, not quite a memory—more of a story that I've heard so many times from so many different family members that it has *become* a memory to me.

It was the Christmas when I was two years old. In those days I was the only child and grandchild on both sides of the family, and so I was spoiled rotten (or so the general consensus of the story goes; my degree of "spoiled" actually depends upon who is telling me the story). Because I was the only child that year, December 25, 1974, was going to be a busy day for me, and I had several different holiday parties I was expected to attend. I was like a preschool socialite. My parents and my extended family had divided up my gifts between all the parties so I'd have something to open at each home. God forbid I arrived at Great-Aunt Arabella's house with nothing to open. The horror! My Christmas would be absolutely ruined! (I told you my mother was an overachiever.)

We got about halfway through the day and I was at the house of some great-aunt or second cousin, or something like that, when I apparently became Jenni-zilla. After opening gifts nonstop for hours I was finally through the first couple of waves. I sat by the Christmas tree, surrounded by piles of Barbie dolls, mounds of art supplies, stacks of books, tons of baby dolls, and more. I looked like some precious Norman Rockwell painting when I realized something was amiss. Looking around at my booty, I quickly understood that I'd been shortchanged. Something was missing, but what was it? I couldn't put my finger on it. I started going through my list in my head:

- ☑ Barbies. *(Check.)*
- ☑ Art supplies. *(Check.)*
- ☑ Baby dolls—the one that poops *and* the one that cries. *(Check, check.)*
- ☑ Blocks. *(Check.)*
- ☑ Stuffed animals. *(Check.)*
- ☑ Books. *(Check.)*
- ☑ Underwear and socks. *(Ugh. Check, check.)*

And then I *knew*.

I sat up straight, glared at my parents, and demanded loudly: "Hey! Where's my McDonald's?"

Earlier in the month I had made my wish list, and along with Barbies, art supplies, and a shit ton of other stuff, I had asked my parents for a kick-ass Playskool McDonald's. It was not under the tree, and I was more than a little pissed off.

Little did I know that my grandparents had actually bought the Playskool McDonald's and it was waiting for me at the last party as sort of the grand finale of the day. They wanted to save the best for last and see my sweet little face erupt in pure joy and amazement at the miracle of Christmas gifts. Instead, according to family legend, I went nuclear on everyone. I demanded the McDonald's and cried and threw myself on the floor in a fit of screams when it wasn't immediately produced. This temper tantrum was not the reaction my parents had anticipated.

My parents were horrified that their precious snowflake could be such a little bitch. I was promptly put in time-out. I'm not sure if I was able to open my McDonald's that day, because I was such a little shit, but since I remember playing with it, I'm pretty sure I wasn't denied too long. Surely by New Year's I was living my dream of one day working at a McDonald's.

(Side note: I may not remember the day I received my McDonald's, but I do remember playing with this toy. A *lot*. It had little people that didn't have arms, so you had to shove their tray of Big Macs and fries in a slot under their chin. How appropriate, right? Who needs hands when you can snarf your food from a tray wedged under your neck? There was also a merry-go-round for the armless people to play on—which is just silly, since arms are pretty important on a merry-go-round. For those of you born after about 1990, let me explain what a merry-go-round is, because apparently your parents outlawed this fantastic invention. Fucking helicopter parents. A merry-go-round was a wonderful device that spun children around with absolutely no safety precautions whatsoever. The object of the game was to hold on tightly until the strength in your hands gave out and you went flying off the contraption, usually onto a concrete playground, or hold on until you puked all over the merry-go-round, which resulted in you being called names and being ostracized for the rest of the day. Either way you had a blast! You can thank your asshole parents for denying you this insanely fun toy. Ask them about teeter-totters, too. Ask them if they have trust issues from being the kid up top when their so-called friend hopped off the bottom seat and let them crash to the ground. Sure, a few kids got hurt now and then, but come on, you can barely see the scars on my face anymore! These kinds of playground toys just kept us on our toes and made us wily. Shit, by the time Adolpha and Gomer have kids, I'm guessing swings and slides will have been outlawed and will be nothing but distant memories, too.)

Anyway, back to my McDonald's pseudo-memory. This tale has been passed down over the years, and even family members who weren't there love to tell me what an asshole I was that day. It's practically become folklore in our family. It's a cautionary tale told to pregnant cousins around a campfire. Who relishes recounting their favorite holiday story of the day their niece or granddaughter was a tyrannical, out-of-control toddler? My family, that's who.

When is it ever a good idea to say to your cousin, "Oh yeah, I heard about your breakdown. You're famous in our house. My parents decided right then and there to delay having kids for another ten years or so"?

This explains why I am six years older than my nearest cousin. It's almost like our own Aesop's fable.

I became infamous. I became That Kid. The one who throws a massive fit on Christmas Day like a spoiled little brat.

Now that I'm a mother (who watches so much TLC that I've become numb from seeing scores of bratty kids go ballistic every day), I can sympathize with my parents. They were trying to make the day extra special for me, but they didn't really think it through and so they never saw the blowup coming. They thought that at two years old, I was a big girl and I could handle it. They thought that by spacing out the presents it wouldn't be as over-whelming for me and in the end it would be more fun for me. They thought that scheduling three or four back-to-back dog-and-pony shows where I was the main attraction wouldn't cause a problem—after all, I loved being the center of attention! Right? (Yeah, usually.) *Smile for Great-Uncle Joe, Jenni! Show us your presents!* (Too bad Great-Uncle Joe didn't realize my parents didn't have a working camera. He could have sent those pictures to us and then I'd know if this story is true.)

What they forgot is that the age of two is when you finally start to notice that there are fun things *inside* the boxes that you enjoyed playing with last year. They forgot that two is when you can talk and have an opinion on what you want for Christmas. Plus, a two-year-old kid has a memory like an elephant. They forgot that two is when you *seem* mature enough to take on a day full of endless celebrations with no nap in sight and a seemingly unending supply of fun and presents, but you're really not. They forgot that two is when you are smart enough to look around and realize what's missing, but you don't have the social skills to ask nicely and casually about your missing present. Instead, you behave like a raving lunatic junkie who hasn't been fed anything all day except cheese and candy (because you refuse to put down your new presents and have a goddamned piece of turkey) and are looking for your next fix.

To this day, if people in my extended family ask for a special gift for Christmas and they don't get it, they will announce loudly, "Hey! Where's my McDonald's?" and then laugh like maniacs.

This story is so popular with my entire family that once a cousin bought his wife a beautiful piece of jewelry she'd been hinting for all year. He waited until all of the presents were opened. He could tell his wife was a little bummed when she realized her bracelet wasn't under the tree like she'd hoped. She tried to put on a brave face, but he could tell she was disappointed. He went into the other room and returned with a crumpled McDonald's bag (with the bracelet inside), threw it in her lap, and said, "Hey! Here's your McDonald's!"

THE WHITE TRASH DOLLHOUSE

When I was nine I asked Santa for a dollhouse for Christmas. This was probably the last year I was going to believe in Santa, and my mother wanted to keep the magic alive for as long as possible, since C.B. was only five.

I don't know exactly how the conversation between my parents went, so I'm going to take some artistic license and assume it went something like this:

Mom: Jenni wants a dollhouse from Santa this year. She's beginning to ask a lot of questions. We need to make this happen or else she'll tell C.B. that Santa isn't real.

Dad: Do you have any idea how much work a dollhouse is? I saw the Barbie Dream House on sale in Sunday's paper—let's just get her that.

Mom: Absolutely not! *That* is not a dollhouse. That's a piece of crap where that bimbo entertains her gay boyfriend in the rooftop hot tub.

Dad: So, what are you thinking?

Mom: When I was a girl, I always wanted an authentic wooden dollhouse with a couple of bedrooms, a living room, and a kitchen, plus an attic nursery. I always wanted my dad to build me one, but he never had time.

Dad: Is this *your* dream house or Jenni's?

Mom: Trust me. It's what *every* little girl wants. Look, it's not a big deal, we could ask my dad to do it, no problem.

Dad: Excuse me? *I* am Jenni's father. If anyone's going to make her a dollhouse, it will be me!

Mom: Well, you're so busy with work, I just thought you'd prefer to have my dad make it. Plus, he's so much better at—

Dad: At what? Building things? I have power tools, you know. Your father and mother gave them to me as a wedding gift. I'm pretty sure they're still in the garage in their boxes. I know how to build a stupid dollhouse! In fact, *my* dollhouse will kick every other dollhouse's ass.

Mom: I don't think dollhouses have asses.

Dad: Mine will have wallpaper and wall-to-wall shag carpet.

Mom: I don't think shag is popular anymore.

Dad: I will even build a little doghouse that matches the big house. Just you wait and see!

Mom: That sounds great. It's just that it's already October . . . you might want to start this weekend.

Dad: Would you leave the planning to me, please? You get the furniture for the house and I'll build it. I'll have it done ahead of schedule and under budget! Now, if you'll excuse me, I have a nap to take!

For the next several weeks my dad spent many late nights at his office building my dollhouse. Because this was supposed to be a gift from Santa, my parents couldn't tell us why our dad was working so late at night. My mom would let me and C.B. call him to say goodnight and we'd act like total shitheads. We'd cry and beg him to come home. We'd tell him about all the fun he was missing (as if missing my mother's Taco Frito Surprise casserole was worth pining for—he dodged that bullet happily) and basically do whatever we could to make him feel like a terrible dad. (Side note: Are you catching on to the recurring theme here about my childhood? I was a bit of a whiny bitch who liked to ruin people's nice surprises. I'm still that way. Don't try to surprise me with anything. Tell me what you're doing so I can be properly grateful and not act like a total douchebag.)

Finally it was Christmas Eve, and I can only imagine the excitement my parents were experiencing that night when my dad crept through our quiet house with my dollhouse and put it in the living room, smack dab in front of the tree.

Dad: Jenni is going to flip out when she sees this!

Mom: Hmm, it seems like something is missing . . .

Dad: No. It's fine.

Mom: No, I'm pretty sure it's missing something.

Dad: Okay. Yeah, I know. I didn't quite get the doghouse done, but I figured Jenni might enjoy doing that one herself. *[The doghouse was four bare plywood walls—no siding, not even a coat of paint—glued to a plywood base with a peaked plywood roof and a rounded opening for the dog.]*

Mom: Well, it seems like it's more than just the doghouse. . . .

Dad: Right. The roof still needs some finishing touches. *[The roof was made of tiny, individual wood shakes that needed to be glued on one at a time. An entire row was missing, and* a few had gotten broken in transit from the office to the house. I'm assuming Dad ran out of shingles and couldn't remember where he bought them in the first place, so he couldn't find any that matched. Also, I'm sure he didn't feel like he could ask his secretary to run out on Christmas Eve and find him another bag of shingles for just one row and a stupid doghouse.]

Mom: And the porch . . . *[It was supposed to be covered with tiny, individual paving stones that connected together and then were attached with wood glue. The porch was still plywood with no bricks at all.]*

Dad: Yeah, but who really notices a porch when you've got wall-to-wall carpeting? *[The dollhouse did have wall-to-wall beige carpet and wallpaper throughout. These are my dad's specialties even in real houses. In fact, there were different wallpaper patterns in each room that were remnants from the house we lived in. So the dollhouse kitchen matched my mother's kitchen, the dollhouse master bedroom matched theirs, and so on.]*

Mom: I guess so . . . How are we going to tell Jenni that Santa didn't get her dollhouse finished?

Dad: What do you mean? It's finished! It has carpet and wallpaper!

Mom: Well, it's not exactly finished. Santa would never call this finished.

Dad: Fine. His elves went on strike before it could get done?

Mom: Hardly.

Dad: Y'know what? Screw Santa! Let's just tell her the truth. I've worked my ass off on the damn thing and I'd appreciate a little credit! Why does he get all the glory? I'm the one who built this thing. I won't even get a thank-you tomorrow. It will all be Santa, Santa, Santa!

Mom: We can't! She'll never be able to keep it from C.B.!

Dad: Well then, what do you suggest?

Mom: I don't know. Can't you finish it now?

Dad: Are you kidding me? It's midnight. No. Forget it! Either she gets it like it is or she doesn't get it at all.

Mom: But all her other gifts from our family are furniture for this stupid house! Her Christmas will be ruined! *[Another recurring theme in my childhood—the looming prospect of ruined Christmases.]*

Dad: Well, my entire month has been ruined working on this stupid fucking thing. You decide. I'll leave it here or stick it back in the car. Choose now.

The next morning C.B. and I flew down the stairs to see what Santa had brought us. My mother waited at the bottom of the stairs with her crappy camera (shocker—it was "out of the shop" that year, probably so she could photograph C.B.) to capture our reactions on film. (Remember, kids, these were the days before digital cameras or cameras on your phone—hell, these were the days before cell phones, forget phones that took pictures! That was some *Star Trek* shit when I was nine years old.) I saw my dollhouse and squealed with delight until my mother blinded me with the flash on the camera. Between my long flannel *Little House on the Prairie*-inspired nightgown and the flash, I almost fell down the stairs.

I regained my footing as my mother yelled at me, "Go back and do it again, Jenni!"

"Huh?" I asked.

"Go back. And do it. Again," she said slowly, like I had actually hit my head. "The flash didn't go."

"Yes it did. It blinded me," I whined. I kept looking at my dollhouse. I just wanted to get down there and see it up close.

"Well, even if it did, I'm pretty sure you blinked. It's going to be a terrible picture. Start at the third stair from the top. Just come down again and give me a big 'Wow!'" my mother said impatiently.

"What about me, Mommy?" asked C.B.

"I think you were okay, but Jenni ruined the picture and I want you both in it. Go up there with her."

C.B. and I trudged to the third stair from the top and turned and started down again.

"Holy cow!" C.B. yelled, and pointed.

"Ohhh . . . myyyy!" I exclaimed in slow motion.

My mother shot a picture, advanced the film, shot another, advanced the film, and shot another.

By now we were at the bottom of the stairs and bursting with excitement to see what Santa had left us.

"I think you got it, dear," my dad said, taking the camera from her hands.

My mother actually did my father a favor that day. Because I was still seeing spots from all the flash photography, I barely noticed the dilapidated roof or the white-trash porch on my dollhouse. I was just so excited to get it, I didn't care about the condition it was in.

"Hey, Jenni, do you like your dollhouse?" my dad asked me later that day.

"Oh yeah!" I replied.

"I noticed it still needs some work to be done," he said.

"Really?" I asked.

"Yeah. Not much, though. Santa told me he thought you might like to do it yourself—with my help, of course."

"Oh yeah?" I said.

"Yeah. I think he knows how independent you are, and he wanted you to have some of the fun building the house, too. This way it can be exactly like you want it. You want my help?"

"Sure!" I said.

"Great. We'll work on it today . . . right after my nap. Okay?"

"Sounds great, Dad!"

To this day, the dollhouse sits in my parents' attic with a mangled roof, an unfinished porch, and a dilapidated doghouse.

LIKE A NEON VIRGIN IN GUESS JEANS AND SWATCH WATCHES

The Christmas I was twelve is commonly referred to as the "Neon Christmas." I was in junior high and artists like Madonna and Cyndi Lauper were all the rage. Every girl in America wanted to be them. My dad took one look at Madonna on MTV and called her a "hooker who would never last." Ha. Looks like Madonna and her crazy, creepy, super-toned fifty-plus-year-old arms are having the last laugh, Dad!

That was also the year I became a label whore and fashion victim all at the same time. Up until that point I had been in private school and had to wear a uniform to school every day, so I never got to cut loose and embrace a fad. On the weekends, I pretty much wore whatever my mother picked out for me: silly tops with my initials embroidered on Peter Pan collars, corduroy vests (sometimes with rainbow suspenders and sometimes without), snazzy velour track suits, and homemade jumpers. You name the bad look, I wore it.

In 1985, I left private school and hopped the school bus to a public New Jersey junior high. For that first day of school, I tossed my terrible past fashion faux pas out the window and joined the MTV nation with my industrial-sized can of Aqua Net, a pair of acid-washed jeans, and a fashionably ripped T-shirt. I had purchased the jeans and T-shirt at the local mall but had foolishly disregarded the labels on these clothes. To me, one pair of acid-washed jeans was just like any other pair. Silly, silly, stupid Jenni!

Luckily, my peers at public school quickly educated me. I found a group of girls who took me under their collective giant Jersey-girl bangs—I mean wings—and explained to me that I was totally grody to the max.

Julie: Oh. My. God. Like, what are you wearing?

Me: Acid-washed jeans.

Julie: Yeah, but from *where*? What brand are those? Those are not Guess!

Me: No, they're not. I think I bought them at Deb. They're, like, half the price of Guess.

Carrie: Ewww. Gag me with a spoon! Of course they're, like, half the price! Deb is totally for burnouts and hosers.

Andi: No, I think your jeans are really bitchin' . . . Sike!

Carrie: Burn!

Me: I didn't know. I came from private school.

Andi: Oh, thank God. That makes so much more sense. I thought maybe you were SPED.

Me: SPED?

Julie: Duh. Special ed. Did you ride the short bus today?

Me: Oh. Uh, no. It was a fairly big bus, actually.

Andi: No shit, Sherlock. We ride the same bus.

Julie: Look, you're not a complete loss. Your jeans are bogus and your shirt is just . . . ick. Your bod is sort of okay, but we can fix you.

Me: You can?

Andi: Totally! You should have seen Carrie last year. She was so grody! Everyone wanted to put a bag over her head until we got hold of her.

Carrie: Now I'm, like, totally rad.

Me: You do look . . . rad.

Julie: No duh!

Andi: Do you want to be fixed?

Me: Of course!

Andi: We have to hit the Livingston Mall, because the Morris County Mall is always crawling with mall maggots.

Julie: Do you have access to a credit card?

Me: I'm not sure. I mean, my mom has one. She usually goes shopping with me.

Carrie: We need to be able to shop in total freedom. No parental units.

Me: Okay, I guess I could ask if I could use her card.

Andi: We find it's better to just borrow the card and then return it at a later date. The parental unit rarely notice that a card's even missing.

Julie: Unless someone totally narcs on you.

Me: Um . . . that's okay. Yeah, I'll just ask my mom. She'll totally say yes, she's . . . uh . . . gnarly like that.

Julie: Don't call your mom gnarly, that's so weird.

Me: Right.

Carrie: Ugh. Like, what is your damage?

Julie: Totally! You're such a noid!

Andi: All right, guys, take a chill pill. That's enough baggin' on Jenni for today. She's our special project. We can't be mean to her. We're helping her. Remember? It's not her fault that she dresses like a troll. You *do* own some neon, right?

Me: Neon? Uh . . . No, I don't.

Julie: You've *got* to get some. Madonna wears neon. It's totally bad!

Carrie: Look, first things first. We need to get you a pair of Guess jeans—real ones this time—and some neon, and then you'll need some of those rubber bracelets that Madonna wears.

Julie: Like, don't forget her hair!

Carrie: Yeah, nice head. We should totally get some scrunchies and get your hair off your face.

Andi: Is that a perm?

Me: Yeah, my mom thought it was a good idea.

Carrie: Well, it wasn't.

Andi: You need a Swatch, too!

Me: I have a watch. I got it a few years ago. It's got Mickey Mouse on it, but I wear it ironically. Y'know?

Carrie: Ironic Mickey Mouse? Negatory.

Julie: You need four Swatches, actually. So you can have two on each arm. That's a totally righteous look.

Andi: I'm so sure! Totally.

Carrie: What about miniskirts?

Julie: Not with those legs. We'll get her some stirrup pants.

Andi: No doubt!

Me: That sounds . . . tubular.

Julie: Seriously, Jenni, stop that. You sound like a total spaz.

Me: Bite me, Julie.

Carrie: Ooh . . . face!

Andi: Bell's ringing. We need to book.

Carrie: Yup. Time to bounce.

Julie: Let's jam.

Me: Um . . . ciao!

All: Stop it, Jenni! You're so weird!

Julie, Andi, and Carrie gave me such sage advice that day. I knew exactly what I had to do. I couldn't steal my mom's credit card, so instead I asked my family for clothes that Christmas. The more labels the better, the more neon the better, the trendier the better.

Word spread quickly from one grandparent to the next and trickled down to the aunts and uncles: *Jenni is a hot mess, but there's hope.* My family took it upon themselves to raise my cool factor. They hit their local malls and bought anything they could find that was neon and/or acceptable name brands. That Christmas I received the following:

- One pair Guess jeans. (I was—and still am—very short, and there was only one style of Guess jeans that fit me properly. I'm thinking they were supposed to be capris, but capris hadn't caught on yet. I didn't care—all I knew was there was an upside-down triangle on my ass and I didn't have six-inch cuffs on my pant legs. I was thrilled.)
- Four neon sweatshirts—yellow, green, orange, and pink.
- Five Limited sweaters that hung off one shoulder. (Yes, it was a bit chilly in the winter, but I was too cool to notice.)
- Three neon purses—one green and two orange.
- Three Swatch watches.
- Approximately twenty neon scrunchies—all colors, many repeats.

Within six months I was completely out of style again. That's when I adopted the signature look that I still sport today: earth-tone cargo pants, black shirts, and sensible shoes. I vowed to never be trendy again, and as most of my friends and family can tell you, I've kept that vow for over twenty-five years.

THE DREADED
ANNUAL CHRISTMAS PHOTO

For as long as I can remember, my mother has always made us pose for an annual family Christmas portrait. She does this so that she can include a copy with her annual Christmas letter to friends and family. I use the word *portrait* loosely. Never once did she trot us off to Olan Mills or even Sears Portrait Studio to have a professional snap us. Instead she'd wait until we were at some family gathering anytime between Halloween and early December, and then she'd ask whichever random relative who had the misfortune of sitting too close to us to take our picture. Nine times out of ten someone's head was cut off or the picture was off-kilter or the focus was off. My mother would ask this poor sap to take "a few" just to make sure she had enough to choose from.

As I got older, my mother's pictures became more elaborate. She liked us to coordinate our look so that we blended together. I don't know what the deal was, but it seemed like everyone else got the style memo but me. My parents and brother would be in navy or red, and I'd show up in orange. We also had to have amazing backdrops. Gone were the days of Grandma or Grandpa snapping a pic of us on our front porch just before they drove away. Now we had to be in front of a roaring fire with stockings behind us or arranged by height on a garland-and-tinsel-shrouded staircase.

I have no clue why anyone (myself included) does this. Who really saves these pictures? Who receives the Punch family portrait and puts it on the refrigerator? Better yet, who thinks: *Oh, wonderful! The Punch family photo has arrived! I am so glad I went ahead and bought that frame the other day. Now I can keep this picture for all time!* No one, that's who. Everyone who receives the Punch family portrait looks at it and says, *Huh, Jen must be looking old since the Hubs used the soft-focus technique this year.* Or even worse: *Just the kids this year? What gives? There must be trouble in paradise. I'm not surprised. Jen has always been a bitch to live with. Poor Hubs—good for him for giving her the heave-ho.*

I know that the only picture I ever save is the one that C.B. and his wife, Ida, send, because I'm actually related to them and I don't mind putting them on my fridge. I would feel awkward gazing into the faces of my hairdresser and her family every morning when I get out the milk. I've never even met her husband and I didn't know she had kids until she sent the picture. So the hairdresser's picture joins everyone else's in the pile that sits on my counter for a week or so while I contemplate saving them for some stupid project I found on Pinterest. And then I realize, who am I kidding? There is no way in hell I am *ever* going to use my cell phone to take a picture of someone's Christmas portrait and save it in my phone as the picture that comes up when they call me. (I'm exhausted just thinking about it, so there's no way I would actually *do* that!) Nor will I ever punch a hole in the upper left-hand corner of each picture or card so that

I can thread them all together with precious holiday ribbon and make an adorable coffee-table keepsake flip book.

Nope, I just like to see how old, bald, fat, or thin everyone has gotten over the years and how big the kids are now and then I toss the cards in the recycle bin because I care about our planet.

But here is my dirty little secret. While I'm hardly a Christmas overachiever, when it comes to holiday cards I make my own family do the same thing. We sit in front of our "good" tree or our fireplace with the stockings behind us (my mother was right—a roaring fire *does* look better than a cold, dark hearth). I dictate the wardrobe, which is usually red and black, since the Hubs and I look best in black (so slimming!) and the kids can be our splash of color in their red. We set the timer on the camera and I make the Hubs take many, many shots since he and Adolpha can't smile naturally. When they try to smile naturally, they both look like absolute freaks with huge teeth and dead eyes. It's a frightening combination.

When I was a child, if my lack of style wasn't enough to make me stand out in these pics, my hairdos made sure I wasn't overlooked. I have naturally curly hair that tends to do whatever it wants. Back in the 1970s and '80s, when I was growing up, there wasn't much you could do for my type of hair. Nowadays, however, there are amazing products that smooth and condition unruly hair. There are shampoos and creams and gels that make your curls nicer or tame them into straight, glistening sheets. Not so much back then. Flatirons didn't exist, or if they did, I didn't know about them—but I wish I had, because the flatiron has literally changed my life.

Back then everyone was obsessed with "feathering" and there was no way in hell my hair was going to feather, ever. It was always frizzy, dry, and limp. I could get one side to feather brilliantly, but the other side stuck straight out because I had fucked-up cowlicks. For real. My mother wasn't much help in this department, as she had her own hair problems. Her hair is thick and coarse, and by the time she was done fighting it into submission I think she was too exhausted to mess with mine.

When I was six I had long hair that I had worn in Laura Ingalls–style braids for years. That year I cut them off for the Dorothy Hamill 'do, thinking maybe short hair would cooperate better. Alas, one side flipped under beautifully, while the other side flipped up. *Son of a bitch!*

That's when someone (I'm assuming my mother) decided that a perm would be the solution to all of my problems. A fucking perm. What the hell was she thinking? I blame my mother, but she swears it was me who begged for a perm. I have no idea. All I know is that someone sensible should have stopped this.

When I brought the Hubs home for the first time and he saw the Christmas picture circa 1983, he said, "Oh God! Look at your hair!"

"Yeah," I replied. "Everyone calls that 'Jenni's pube-head phase.'"

DOESN'T EVERYONE WRAP CHRISTMAS PRESENTS IN THEIR UNDERWEAR?

Growing up, I was not the sharpest tool in the shed when it came to math and geography, but this was especially true when it came to sex. When my mother finally sat me down and told me about the birds and the bees, my initial reaction, like that of many kids my age, was disgust.

"Ewww," I said with a grimace. And then I saw my brother, C.B., and my superior math skills kicked in. I did the addition (in my head, thank you very much), which made me even more grossed out. "Hold on. You mean you did that twice? Double ewww."

I was thoroughly revolted, but I could handle the idea of my parents getting busy as long as I thought sex was for procreation only. The thought of sex for recreation would not occur to me for many more years. (It's actually embarrassing just how many years it took for me to think of that idea.) What I'm trying to say is the thought never crossed my mind that my parents might actually *enjoy* their . . . *ahem* . . . alone time. (Triple ewww—the thought still makes me squirm a little.) So it was a huge surprise to me when I finally came to that realization.

When I was a kid my dad had a job that forced him to be on the road Monday through Friday, so the weekends were when my parents caught up with each other. It had been a *loooong* five days for Dad, living in a hotel room and surviving on whatever he could get out of a vending machine. It had been an even longer five days for Mom, shuttling C.B. and me around town, mediating hourly disputes over who exactly was touching whom, nagging us to clean our rooms, and helping us with our homework. I'm guessing she would have killed for an empty hotel room, fully stocked vending machines, and a mini-bar, but this isn't a competition to see who had it the worst (even though Mom totally did). We all missed Dad during the week, and C.B. and I were glad to see his suitcase in the front hall every Friday after school. Mostly because it meant that Mom would cook something besides eggs or Frito pie for dinner. Breakfast for dinner is only a fun treat when it doesn't happen *every* Monday night.

As soon as we saw Dad, C.B. and I would try to tell him everything he'd missed during the week. Since I was the oldest and the loudest, I'd always start. "Dad, Dad, Dad! There was this girl at lunch on Wednesday. She's new and she is so cool. She has the best Guess jeans! They're a brand-new style. No one in Jersey has them yet! Her grandma sent them to her from New York City or something. But my friend Kerry, she has an older sister who works at the mall, she said her sister's store is getting like two pairs on Saturday, but she can only hold a pair of them for me until noon. Can I have some money? I *need* to get those Guess jeans or else no one will like me!"

"Dad, Dad, Dad!" C.B. would interject. "Jenni doesn't need any more jeans, and we all know more jeans aren't going to help Jenni get new friends. She'll still be a weirdo—just a weirdo with new jeans. Nothing can help that. But *I* need a new skateboard. Mine broke this week while you were gone. Mom says I can't have a new one because I was messing around when it broke, but it wasn't my fault that it broke. It wasn't good quality. If I had a decent board, it would have never broken when I tried to grind with it. A decent board would have grinded perfectly."

"Isn't the word *ground*, C.B.? And stop calling me a weirdo, weirdo. Look, it doesn't matter, Dad. Who cares about the jeans? What I *really* need is a telephone in my room. *Everyone* has their own phone and their own phone line. It actually makes a lot of sense, because then I won't tie up Mom's phone with my calls. I got in super-big trouble this week for talking on the phone too much, so Mom took away my phone privileges because she totally missed like eight calls from Grandma. She finally reached her and it wasn't like it was an emergency or anything—she was just calling to chat! If I had my own phone line, that would never happen. Oh! I'll also need three-way calling, call waiting, and a fifty-foot cord so I can take the phone everywhere. It's essential."

"She's getting a phone? Are you serious? If Jenni gets her own phone line, do I get one, too? It's only fair."

My dad would eat his meal without saying much. He'd simply nod along while C.B. and I harangued him and bled his wallet dry. I'm guessing his behavior was the result of a combination of guilt for missing an entire week of our lives and our patented method of relentless whining. Fifty dollars for jeans probably seemed like a decent price for a meal that wasn't a Snickers bar washed down with a can of Pepsi.

My mom didn't nag Dad too much, but she also didn't shush me and C.B. She had put up with our crap all week, and I'm sure she felt like it was his turn to listen to us.

Dad would use Friday night to decompress and get back in

the groove of being home, and on Saturday C.B. and I would have our dad's attention for most of the day. He would play games or watch TV with us. Sometimes he'd take the family to the movies or out to dinner.

However, Sunday was a whole other story. We always went to church on Sunday and came home for lunch. After lunch, my parents always retreated to their bedroom, leaving C.B. and me to fend for ourselves. With only one TV to share, fights quickly ensued.

My brother and I have differing memories when it comes to our fights. I remember fighting a lot. He does, too. That's the only memory we have in common. I remember a lot of screeching and yelling and *threatening* of bodily harm. C.B. just remembers actual bodily harm. He could write his own book about how much *alleged* abuse he suffered at my hands. According to him, it's a small miracle he's still alive. Oh, C.B.! He has such an active imagination, you'd have thought he would have been the one to grow up and write half-true books. Instead he has one of the least imaginative jobs out there. He's a CPA.

But I digress. Back to Sundays. On Sundays, my parents would lock themselves in their room and my brother and I would immediately start fighting over what we should watch on television. My brother and I would finally grow tired of *allegedly* beating the crap out of each other, and we'd go looking for our parents to referee.

We always found the door bolted, so we switched from fighting to whining through the tiny crack between the door and the jamb. "Can we come *innnnn*?" C.B. would whine. "Jenni's banging my head into the floor because I won't let her watch MTV."

"Shut up, C.B. That's not true, Mom! C.B. keeps kicking me in the stomach because he thinks I'm on his side of the couch."

We would hear muffled voices on the other side. We'd strain to listen.

"What did you say, Dad? Did you say Jenni should stop hogging the couch?"

We would listen more, but we couldn't understand anything that was being said.

C.B. and I would look at each other and shrug. We couldn't figure out what was going on. What were they doing in there? Why was the door locked? It was never locked any other time except for Sunday afternoons. What was so private in there that we couldn't be a part of it, too?

"Mom? I want to go to Kristie's house. Can I go?" I'd yell.

Muffle, muffle, muffle. Did someone just giggle?

"I want to go to a friend's house, too!" C.B. would yell.

"No!" Mom would yell back. "C.B., you cannot go off on your own, and Jenni, you cannot leave C.B. You are in charge out there! Go find something to do! Go watch HBO! We pay a fortune for it and you should watch it more!"

Dad always chimed in with a totally inappropriate movie suggestion. "They had the HBO guide in my room at the hotel. *Cujo* is on at three today. You guys should go watch it."

Muffle, muffle, muffle. Okay, someone *was* giggling in there!

"*Moooooommmmm,* we're so bored out there. C.B. is being a brat and won't do what he's told. And *Cujo* is totally rated R, Dad. C.B. can't watch that."

"Jenni!" It would be my father this time, using his stern don't-you-dare-talk-back-to-me-young-lady voice. "Listen carefully to me. Your mother just told you to find something to do. Now go do that!"

"*Daaaaddd,* Jenni is being a jerk and she shoved my head into the wall!"

"I did not!"

"You did!"

"Hey!" The door would open just enough for my dad to stick his head through. "Listen to me, you two. You need to get away from this door and go find something to do, because your mother and I need some privacy."

"But why?" I would whine. "What are you guys doing in there?"

"Why are the lights off and the shades closed?"

"Oh my God, Dad, are you in your underwear? Ewww."

"Knock it off, Jenni. Go ride your bikes or something. Your mother and I need to be alone."

"But why?"

"Yeah, why? We want to come in there with you."

"You can't. We're doing something very secret in here."

"What kind of secret? What are you doing in there?"

"We won't tell." C.B. would try to push his way in.

"You can't come in here, because we're . . . we're . . ." We would hear our mother mumble and giggle. Seriously, what was with all the giggling? And then he'd say, "You can't come in because we're wrapping your Christmas presents!"

C.B.'s eyes would light up. "What? Christmas presents? Cool!"

I was a tad more skeptical—at first. "But you're in your underwear, Dad."

"I'm more comfortable in my underwear. I need to be comfortable when I'm wrapping Christmas presents."

"But it's August, Dad."

"That's right! I know it's August, Jenni, but we've got so many presents for you and your brother we have to start wrapping now or else they'll never get done. You know how your mother likes the presents to look extra nice. It takes her a long time to make the packages so pretty. Don't tell your mother I said so, but I think I saw some Guess jeans in a bag in her closet."

That was all it took. My skepticism would flit away as I dreamed of beautifully wrapped packages containing Guess jeans and Princess phones.

"Dad, are you wrapping a skateboard? Because I really need it before December. Maybe I could get it early?"

"Hey! C.B., I'm not telling you what we're wrapping. I'm just telling you that if you want these presents, you'll find something else to do and leave us alone to . . . wrap in peace!"

Well, nothing could motivate us like the thought of presents, so C.B. and I would skedaddle and leave our parents to their very private wrapping sessions.

Never once did it occur to either of us that this excuse was used just as much in August as it was in November. Never once did we think, "Hey . . . wait a minute. They wrap Christmas presents every weekend, but we're lucky if we get ten presents to open on Christmas morning. The math just doesn't add up."

I'd like to thank my parents for scarring me for life by making me forever equate the phrase "I have to wrap some Christmas presents" with "Let's get it on!" I really blame C.B. for this more than myself, because he was the one who was supposedly "gifted." I was the kid who always brought down the class average. No one expected genius from me, but C.B. should have known better.

HEY, SANTA, KEEP YOUR YULE LOG TO YOURSELF!

I was thinking about taking my kids to see Santa today. I always like to get a picture of them dressed up in their good Christmas clothes, and it's usually a hassle to wrangle them out of their jeans and swishy shorts. However, we'd gone to church earlier with my parents, the kids were dressed to kill, and we were near my favorite mall Santa, so it seemed like the perfect opportunity.

I realized, though, it was the Sunday before Christmas and the mall would be a zoo. Ugh. No way did I want to even try to get near that. The kids would be out of school in a couple of days and I could take them then, when the lines *might* be shorter.

I know what you're thinking: *C'mon, Jen, really? You get your kids all dressed up and haul them to the mall to get their picture taken with Santa? I thought you were cooler than that.*

Sorry to disappoint. As I noted earlier, we all have our skeletons in our closet. I'm not perfect.

You must understand, while I am a card-carrying underachiever, I am the daughter of an overachiever. I am a total deadbeat and a major disappointment to my mother when it comes to Christmas. But a few traditions, like the "nice" Santa picture and the annual Christmas letter, have rubbed off on me. We *do* share DNA, after all.

When we were growing up, my mother *always* took my brother and me to get our picture taken with Santa. It didn't matter how rich or poor my parents were at the time—by God, we were budgeting for that Santa picture!

There isn't a picture of me crying on Santa's lap, because my parents thought that was cruel. By the time C.B. came along, they decided it was perfectly fine to photograph their crying baby on a strange man's lap. I think that one might be my favorite.

Every Christmas my mom puts our pictures through the years on display around the house so we can see how adorable we once were. How sad is it that I peaked at age four?

So, here is my face, an arm, and my hand testing the waters with Snoopy.

These photos were so embarrassing growing up (the hairstyles, the clothes), and I feel it's only fair that now I get to inflict the same pain and suffering on my children. It's these little things that bring me joy during the holidays.

As C.B. and I got older, this tradition still continued. We *hated* going to see Santa and getting our pictures taken. We would whine and fuss, but my mother would insist and my father would yell at us to "do something nice for your mother for once," so off we'd go.

Once I hit thirteen, I was able to convince my mother that she really only needed C.B. in the photo. I also made sure that she noted my age, because I didn't want him to finagle his way out of the Santa picture before he was thirteen. I'd had to endure it for a full thirteen years, and so should he!

My mother was devastated that I wouldn't do the picture anymore, but she didn't fight me on it. I think she thought I'd see the error of my ways and come around eventually. Boy, was she wrong.

I'm not sure when it happened, but at some point before he was thirteen, my brother was let out of his commitment. There is one year where the picture is of just my mom and my dad on Santa's knee!

My first Christmas break home from college, I told C.B. it would be funny if we went to the mall and got a picture with Santa. I didn't have a real present for my mom, and I thought a twelve-dollar picture would be worth more than any expensive gift I didn't want to buy. I told my brother he'd have to split the cost with me if he wanted credit for the present. (Those photos are pricey, and I wasn't going to let him get credit if he didn't cough up the dough.)

We hit the "popular mall" on Christmas Eve and the Santa line was outrageous, so we decided to try the "gross mall." You know the gross mall—it's the one that no one really goes to. Every town has one. Ours was a semi-abandoned mall with two anchor stores and about five open stores throughout the middle of the mall. The rest of the storefronts were literally boarded up. We were sure the lines would be so much shorter, because we didn't think any of the über-moms would deign to go to that mall with their precious pumpkins. We, on the other hand, could care less.

The line was about what we expected—a few exhausted and stressed-out moms who were trying to make memories (damn it) without having to wait six hours at the good mall.

We got in line and waited our turn.

When we got up to Santa, I took one look at him and nearly backed out of the deal.

My mother had never taken us to see the gross mall Santa. I have childhood memories of going to see Santa where we waited something like eight hours (or so it seemed) in a winter wonderland maze on the top floor of Macy's flagship store in New York City. I remember being so hot from all the twinkling lights and having minor panic attacks about locating fire exits, because I was sure those lights would somehow short out and cause the place to blaze up. I can remember having to pee so badly and being trapped in the line with no hope of a "chicken exit" for the bathroom. I can remember happy, borderline-maniacal "elves" asking my parents if we had any "special needs" *(Yes, a cup to pee in!)* and telling us, "The wait's not much longer now. You're *almost* to the North Pole!" and then we'd turn the corner and see *miles* of people still ahead of us. *Liars! I'm going to wet myself and I'm wearing my nice Christmas outfit!* When we finally got into the little cottage to see Santa, he was a good-looking St. Nick with rosy cheeks, a real beard, a big tummy, and a pricey costume. Macy's hired pros. Once, the Santa we got could even speak English to me and C.B. and French to our friends who had just moved to the States. We *all* believed for another year after that one!

The Santa at the gross mall was nothing like the Macy's Santa. He was a dirty mall Santa like none other.

He was skinny. Like meth-head skinny. Who hires a skinny Santa? The gross mall does.

His beard was real, but it was yellow.

His hair was gray, but it was lank and filthy.

His costume was worn out on the thighs where the kids sit, and the white fluffy parts were dingy and gray.

He took one look at me and smiled—actually, I believe the

word is *leered*—then patted his bony thighs and said something to the effect of "Have a seat, sugar."

We went up to him and I said, "We're too big to sit down on your lap. We'll just sort of perch." I tried to sit on the armrest of his chair, but I was too short to get up there *and* keep my feet on the floor (damn you, giant overstuffed chairs), so I sort of crouched and hovered over his scrawny legs, refusing to actually sit down on his cootie-infested pants. I about puked when I saw he was sporting wood. "Oh God! Take the picture—quickly!" I yelled.

In the photo, my brother is laughing like a hyena, and I look like I just got my ass pinched by a mall Santa with a boner.

Because I did.

I didn't do anything about it, though. I was all of eighteen years old and was not the spitfire I am today. Instead, I gritted my teeth, paid for my picture (the *hell* I was going to go back for a retake), and decided my mother would never get another Santa picture from me again.

If this had happened today, I would *own* that mall Santa's meth-lab car *and* his trailer home.

The sad irony is now that I am older and bitchier and wouldn't stand for that crap, there will never be another time that a gross mall Santa will even *want* to grab my ass. And let's face it, I'm so old now that if he did, I'd probably just be flattered.

Making My Own Christmas Memories (Note: They Still Suck)

FA-RA-RA-RA-RAA, RA-RA-RA-RAA: MY CHRISTMAS STORY

When December 2001 rolled around, the Hubs and I had been dating for several years. We had weathered our first non-date at the exotic TGIFriday's, and we'd stuck together even though I had worn overalls and he'd warned me before our dinner that if I was boring he'd leave because there was a new episode of *Homicide* on that night.

So while we'd dated for years, our parents had never met. They lived in different cities and had never had the opportunity (or desire) to get together until they found out they would some-day share grandchildren. Then in December 2001 the opportunity for a meeting presented itself. I was working at the latest in my long string of life-sucking jobs in Manhattan and was told that because I'd taken time off for Christmas the year before, I would not be able to have any time off that year and would be expected back in the office on December 26. There was no way I could get home to my parents' house in Kansas for the holiday and be back in New York in time to punch the clock at 9:00 A.M.

I was pretty upset. I had always gone home for Christmas while the Hubs stayed in New York and celebrated the holiday with his family. Now I would be in New York alone for Christmas. Yeah, yeah, the Hubs would be around, but he didn't do Christmas like I was used to.

As much as I make fun of my mother and her shenanigans, her house *feels* like Christmas. The Hubs' family never decorates or even puts up a tree! No tree? WTF? That doesn't feel like Christmas at all. My mom and dad always gave me kick-ass gifts (even if I demanded them or they were half finished). The Hubs' family gives each other socks and underwear for gifts—one year the Hubs gave his mother oatmeal! Those aren't gifts; they're necessities. I would cry if I received socks as my Christmas gift. (Of course, this was before I had children; now I'd be thrilled to get a pair of socks, since the kids get every fucking thing.) No, the Hubs' family was far too practical for me to celebrate with. I'd rather stay home alone than sit around and pretend to be excited watching them open underwear and oatmeal. *"Jockey for Her! Ooh, that's the good stuff. Niiiice."*

C.B. was newly married to Ida and was spending Christmas with her family that year. My parents were going to be alone. I was going to be alone. Of course, my mother couldn't have that. It didn't matter that I was twenty-eight years old—she didn't want me to spend Christmas solo (plus my mother is crazy about New York City at Christmastime, so for her it was a win-win). So the next thing I knew, she and my dad announced they were coming to New York City for Christmas.

In those days I was living in a two-bedroom apartment with limited storage in Forest Hills, Queens. Because of my minimal closet space and the fact that I had always gone home to Kansas City for Christmas, I didn't have any Christmas decorations. I knew my mom would be depressed to begin with because she'd be spending her favorite holiday in my dingy apartment, but if I didn't buy a Christmas tree, she might actually threaten to end her life.

So I turned into an overachieving daughter—but still only half-assed (I can only do so much). I found out many years earlier that I am allergic to evergreen trees. I can't stop coughing, snotting, and sneezing when I'm around those things. My parents had a real Christmas tree for many years and just assumed I was always sick at Christmastime. No one thought, *Gee, there's a pattern here. Maybe we should have Jenni tested for allergies.* Nope. It wasn't until I was older and my mom decided that fake trees were prettier than real trees (and didn't add more time to her daily vacuuming regimen) that we figured out I was allergic. The year my mom came home with a plastic tree, it was the first Christmas when I could breathe through my nose and see out of fully opened eyes. (Yeah, my eyes would swell shut, and *still* no one thought that was at all strange. Way to pay attention, parents.) Because of this, the Hubs and I slogged out to Long Island to pick up a tree and some decorations at Target—and a bin to keep it all in (that was the start of my own Christmas-decoration bin collection). I have no idea what I spent, but I'm sure it was several hundred bucks. The good news is we still have that tree, those ornaments, and that bin, so it was a solid investment.

We put up the tree and planned the meeting of the parents.

The Hubs' parents wanted to spend Christmas Day with us, since I had to work the next day. I thought they would invite us over to their house for a turkey lunch and then we'd play board games all afternoon in front of a toasty fire. I couldn't have been more wrong. Instead, they invited us out to a Chinese restaurant in Flushing, a predominantly Asian section of Queens.

When the Hubs first told me the plan I said, "Won't the restaurants be closed? It's Christmas Day."

He looked at me like I was stupid. "It's Chinese food," he said, as if that simply explained how a restaurant would be open on Christmas Day—a national holiday.

"Okay. What does that have to do with anything?"

"All of Flushing will open. It will be packed."

"On Christmas?"

"Yes."

"But won't people be at home eating turkey?"

"We never eat turkey. We're Chinese. We eat duck," the Hubs replied. "Or Tofurkey."

"So we're going to go to a Chinese restaurant on Christmas to eat Chinese food," I reiterated.

"Yes," the Hubs said, exasperated.

"Will we have Tofurkey?" I asked, not quite sure what that was, exactly.

"No."

"Will we have duck?"

"I don't know. Maybe. It's kind of expensive. My parents won't want to spring for one if you guys won't eat it."

"So . . . we're going to go to a Chinese restaurant on Christmas night to have duck and other kinds of Chinese food? For Christmas dinner?" I said.

"Why is this so hard for you to understand? This is what my family does every year."

"How did I not know this?" I asked.

"I don't know. Probably because you never pay attention to me. Anyway, what does it matter?"

"It just seems strange to me. I am white, y'know. I've never had Chinese food for Christmas dinner. It's funny, though, because it's like that movie," I said.

"What movie?" he asked.

"That movie I love. *A Christmas Story*. The one with the kid who wants a BB gun and everyone says 'You'll shoot your eye out' and stuff," I said.

"I don't know that movie," he replied.

"Of course you do," I reminded him. "The kid is Ralphie and he has glasses and the dogs eat the turkey, so they have to go out for Chinese food on Christmas night."

"Never seen it," said the Hubs, more than a little perturbed with me by now. "Stop saying that I know it, because I don't!"

What? Holy shit! It was like I was engaged to a man I barely knew!

How, after all of these years of dating, had I not known that he went to Flushing on Christmas night to eat Chinese food, and how did he not know the famous *A Christmas Story* movie? I was scared. What else didn't I know?

But then it hit me: he was absolutely right. I didn't pay attention to him. Every year I went home for Christmas, and I would get so caught up seeing friends and family that I wouldn't really have much time to call and chat with him while I was gone. I would call and wish him a merry Christmas, and then I'd head out to a party. He didn't know about *A Christmas Story* because he lived a sad existence in his parents' dank basement in a house without cable. The poor thing had never seen a TBS all-day Christmas marathon of *A Christmas Story*. I couldn't even imagine what that must be like.

One thing was for certain: I couldn't marry a man who didn't know the hysterical beauty that is *A Christmas Story*. It was blasphemy that he'd been alive for so long and had never seen it, and I was determined to fix that.

When my parents finally arrived at my semi-festive Cracker-jack box of an apartment, I told them the plan. "We are going to dinner in Flushing."

"Oh," my mom said. "I didn't think they lived in Flushing."

"They don't. We're going to a restaurant," I said.

"What?" my dad asked. "It will be Christmas night. Nothing will be open! We'd better get a turkey going right now."

"No, Dad," I said. "I've been assured that all of Flushing will be open. We're going to have . . . Chinese food."

"Chinese food?" my mother asked incredulously.

"For Christmas dinner?" my father added.

"Yes," I replied.

"Oh. My. God," my mother said, getting excited. "It will be just like *A Christmas Story*!"

"Yes. Kind of. I guess so," I said.

"Wait. What are you talking about?" my dad asked.

"*Fa-ra-ra-ra-raa, ra-ra-ra-raa*," my mother and I sang together.

"Huh?" my dad said, puzzled.

"*A Christmas Story*—you know that movie. Remember the scene in the movie where they have to eat Christmas dinner at the Chinese restaurant and the waiters sing 'Deck the Halls' with terrible accents?" my mother explained.

"Hopefully they just won't cut a duck's head off at the table in front of us," I said.

"Oh yeah, that movie," my father said. "It's okay. I've always liked *Christmas Vacation* so much better. Now *that's* a good Christmas movie!"

"I have no idea what you guys are talking about," said the Hubs, sounding irritated.

"It's with Chevy Chase," my dad explained to the Hubs. "He's trying to get his Christmas lights up on the house and he goes sledding and his annoying family comes to visit. It is a riot. I'm sure you've seen it."

"No," the Hubs growled. "I haven't."

"Really?" My dad was shocked. "Huh. I thought Jen said you went to film school."

"I did."

"And you've never seen *Christmas Vacation*? That just seems weird to me."

"I don't know what to tell you. We didn't study Christmas movies at NYU film school."

The next day was Christmas. My parents and I got up early and opened our presents. (No socks! Yes!)

My dad just wouldn't let the idea of a turkey dinner go. I'd gotten the damn tree, but he needed a turkey to really feel the complete Christmas vibe. So he got to work preparing a full Christmas dinner with all the fixings while my mom and I introduced the Hubs to the *Christmas Story* all-day marathon.

We settled in on the couch with the Hubs nestled between us and turned on the TV. I have no idea how many times I have seen this movie, but I know it's a lot. I know that I watch it every year—OK, several times every year—and I have many of my favorite lines memorized, including "Fra-jie-lee," so I can recite them out loud at the TV. Mom and I sat there and cackled like a couple of hens while the Hubs watched in near silence.

"Hey! That part was great. Why didn't you laugh?" I asked the Hubs at one point.

"Eh. It wasn't that funny. It was okay," he replied.

"You should watch *Christmas Vacation*!" my dad yelled from the kitchen. "*Much* funnier movie!"

After a disappointing viewing of *A Christmas Story*, we sat down at 1:00 P.M. to eat lunch, knowing full well that we had a

6:00 P.M. reservation with the Hubs' family. As we stuffed our-selves with turkey, mashed potatoes, corn casserole, stuffing, rolls, Jell-O, and whatever else my dad could find in my cup-boards, I reminded them, "We—*chomp, chomp, chomp*—need to be ready to leave in four and a—*gulp, gulp, gulp*—half hours."

"No—*slurp, slurp, slurp*—problem," was the reply I got.

I'm sure it didn't take us that long to eat, but it really felt like we rolled ourselves away from the table just in time to go to Flushing for another huge meal.

The Hubs was right. Flushing was swarming with people. Every restaurant was open for business and bursting at the seams with patrons. It was a good thing the Hubs had made a reservation (even though I'd scoffed at him when he did).

We did have duck that night (along with six other courses), but it came to the table already disassembled (y'know, chopped into ten or so easy pieces) and the head was included on the platter. My future mother-in-law kept trying to get my dad to eat it, while my mom and I waited expectantly for the Chinese wait-ers to sing "Deck the Halls" to us.

Sadly, they never did.

HOARDER'S DELIGHT

OK, so I've already hinted that my mother takes her Christmas decorating very seriously. I just don't know if I can put into words *how* seriously.

To put it lightly, my mother is *insane* when it comes to Christmas. Christmas is not a day. It is an event and a sport as far as she is concerned. And my mother aims to win.

Her Christmas decorations go up as soon as the outside light turns off on Halloween night. Thanksgiving is dead to her—there are not enough adorable turkey decorations to make it worth her while. This woman has been collecting Christmas memorabilia for at least forty years and every single item "has a story." Her words, not mine. Shit, the "stories" my decorations have are something like *I found this beauty in the 70-percent-off bin at the Dillard's after-Christmas sale and I liked how it wasn't broken like everything else in the bin.*

Her Christmas decorations and assorted paraphernalia are stored in more than eighty Rubbermaid totes (eighteen gallons and bigger) that are then stored in the basement or the attic.

The decorating takes her weeks to complete. There is so much that she has to pace herself. She has to start on November 1 so that her home is fully transformed by Christmas.

She literally takes every picture off the wall and replaces it with a Christmas-themed picture (think a rosy-cheeked Santa sneaking up on sleeping kids or snowy watercolor landscapes or an artist's charcoal depiction of Jesus' birth). Her collection of Santas is so large that a few years ago she decided to "keep Christmas alive all year round" and began leaving a few out all the time. Last year she left out her snowman collection on top of her kitchen cabinets. When I mentioned them in February, she said she'd "forgotten" about them. There are fifty snowmen staring at her every morning as she makes coffee—how could she forget about them? (I think she just ran out of steam when she was packing up and didn't want to admit there were too many decorations.) There are so many nativity sets that they have to be seen to be believed. Watch out for the nativities, though: C.B. likes to pose the animals in risqué positions, and it drives my mother bat-shit crazy.

Every dish, cup, bowl, and mug comes out of the cupboard so that it can be replaced with Spode Christmas Tree china. Even the dog gets Christmas bowls to drink and eat from.

Every door handle has a holly-jolly jingle bell dangling from it, and most doors are adorned with wreaths or Advent calendars counting down the days to "C-Day."

Every knick-knack is put away and replaced with ten (or more) Christmas tchotchkes. Books are removed from shelves (no Jackie Collins smut can be out at Christmastime!) and filled with Christmas storybooks, Christmas cookbooks, and a special Christmas memories book that she updates every year to include what we ate for dinner and who got what from Santa. (A quick glance through this book the other day told me that over the years she's made out like a bandit between clothes and jewelry, while C.B. and I managed to get our electronics upgraded every year with new Walkmen, Nintendos, and Discmen. My dad always got a sweater, and sometimes in a good year he got two.)

Most of her decorations, while not my style, are tasteful and cute. It's just the sheer *volume* of Christmas crap that is amazing to me. If I ever need a white-elephant gift or a sweater for an ugly Christmas sweater party, I know exactly where to go. (I bet she'd never even notice anything was missing.)

Every year I give my mom two days of my time to help her decorate her house. This year I wanted to take some pictures of her house so I could share them with you. Because of this, I needed her to put the decorations up in August. I knew it was a lot to ask, so I offered to help her until it was done. I thought, *How hard could it be? It might take another day or so.* Ha!

Holy shit. I had no fucking clue how much work it was going to be. Let me break it down for you by the numbers so you can wrap your brain around my mother's Christmas decorating extravaganza and compare it to my decorating regimen (and keep in mind I'm not even the norm, since I'm a tad overachieving when it comes to holiday decorations):

Mom: Two hundred twenty-five man-hours in labor.

Jen: Twelve man-hours in labor (with breaks for hot cocoa).

Mom: Twelve Christmas trees, ranging from three feet to ten feet high, each with its own theme.

Jen: Six trees, ranging from two feet to twelve feet high (three of which belong to Adolpha). Themes include "Nice Tree—Don't Touch," "Family Tree—Touch Gently," and "Kids' Bedrooms' Trees—Have at It."

Mom: One hundred fifty Santa Claus figures. This number does not include Santa pictures, ornaments, or the like. These are physical, free-standing Santas placed throughout the house.

Jen: Zero Santa Claus figures. WTF? Those are so weird! Plus it looks like someday I stand to inherit seventy-five, so no need to add to my bounty. Actually, I'll probably get them all, since I can't see C.B. showing up to claim his half.

Mom: Three Christmas Villages. I need you to understand just how enormous these villages are. We spent eight of the above-mentioned man-hours unboxing, unwrapping, and placing each of the hundreds of pieces of just one village. This village has ice skaters, penguins, elves, candy shoppes (always with two *p*'s and an *e*), street lamps, picket fences, benches, dogs, ice fishermen, and even a North Pole "fun run." (I don't know about you, but whenever I hear "fun run" I think naked runners. This village does not have naked runners . . . yet. eBay, here I come!)

Jen: One Christmas Village. One day I was shopping with my mom and my aunt Ruby and we saw a village consisting of three tasteful stained-glass buildings that lit up. I remarked, "Now, that's a village I actually like." My mother scoffed, "But where's the rest of the village?" My aunt didn't need to hear another word. She grabbed that sucker and bought it for me. I think she was hoping to get me addicted, but it didn't work. I do put it out every year, but I've never added another village.

Mom: One hundred nineteen snowmen. Like the Santa number, this does not include snowmen on pictures, pillows, or ornaments. This is *actual* snowmen. She has three rooms of her home dedicated to snowmen: (1) the kitchen, where she has an entire forest of snowmen lording over the tops of her kitchen cupboards; (2) the family room, where the snowman tree resides; and (3) the guest bathroom, which looks like a snowman explosion. You can barely take a dump because there isn't much room to work in and it's unsettling to have all those Frosty the Snowmen grinning at you. There are even a few snowmen in the bathtub!

Jen: Five Snowmen. I'm not crazy about snowmen, but I guess I like them better than Santas.

Mom: One hundred two nativity sets. A few years ago I think my mother realized that the "true meaning" of Christmas was getting lost in her villages, snowmen, and Santas, so she decided to start a new collection: nativities. I have to admit, I have added to the madness with gifts such as a blanket emblazoned with a depiction of Christ's birth, because I like to keep it classy.

Jen: Two nativity sets. Each of my kids has a plush nativity they can keep in their rooms during Christmas.

Mom: Twenty-five Spode Christmas Tree china place settings. Are you unsure what this means? That's twenty-five place settings that only come out at Christmastime. Not to mention the serving dishes and utensils that also come out (she actually owns more Christmas-themed serving dishes than regular ones). This year was the first time I helped get them out. Oh. My. God. I wanted to kill myself. I cannot even believe that my mom does this every year. You have to take all of the dishes out of two buffets and all of the kitchen cupboards and move them to the basement. Then you take all of the Christmas china out of the basement and haul it upstairs. WTF! This is insanity. And don't even get me started on the fact that all this shit has to be *washed by hand*. Yup, you can't put it in the dishwasher. Who wants to serve twenty-five people and then wash all the dishes by hand?

Jen: Six Christmas place settings. Back in the day, before I was even engaged to the Hubs, my dad bought me six place settings of my very own Christmas dishes (not Spode, since I get my mother's someday). This was my Christmas present that year. *Gee, thanks, Dad. I would have preferred the cash.* He thought it would be great to have six so that when C.B. and I got married, Ida and the Hubs could each have a dish, too. How awkward is that conversation when you open your present in front of those two and your dad says, "I got you six, Jen, so that when Ida and the Hubs join our family they can eat with us"? No pressure, Ida and Hubs! I've eaten on those dishes once, when I had my parents over for dinner. The rest of the time they sit in the cupboard over the microwave— y'know, the one that is the hardest to get anything out of. I keep telling my dad that I don't get them down because I'm afraid my kids will break them.

Mom: Zero Elfs on the Shelf. My mom is just mad she didn't think of this little bastard first.

Jen: Two Elfs on the Shelf. We have our original, Choppy Elfie, who was a gift from our friends, and I received a second from a reader. We put a skirt on him this year and turned him into a her for Adolpha. We call her Elva the Elf.

I joke that my mother could charge admission to her house. She thinks I'm kidding, but I'm really not. It is a sight to behold and would certainly be worth five bucks for a tour. Hey! I think I just figured out a way for my dad to finally retire! Just put some paper booties on people and let them traipse through your Winter Wonderland! You're welcome, Mom and Dad.

Every year while I'm "fluffing" her trees (not to be confused with porn-star fluffing), I offer to help her thin some of the herd. I make gentle suggestions like, "Seriously, Mom, how many snowman soap dispensers do you need in one bathroom? Couldn't we get rid of two of them, at least?" or "Do you really need Santa waving the American flag and baking gingerbread all at the same time?" or "God, this is so ugly, please chuck it."

My mother can't bear to part with any of her beauties. Every year I make a pile of potential cast-offs, and she goes through them and says things like, "No. Not this. I got this from Gloria. Do you remember her?"

"No."

"Well, I babysat for her son for a few months in 1982, and as payment she gave me this ornament. Whenever I see it I think of Gloria and her son . . . what's his name?"

"Who knows, but Gloria sounds like a real cheap bitch. Who pays a babysitter in Christmas ornaments? If you want to keep it, whatever, I won't argue with you. How about this one? This quilted mouse with a Santa hat and holly-patterned apron that hangs on the wall?"

"No! Our neighbor in Des Moines gave that to me as a hostess gift one year at my Christmas party."

"What was this neighbor's name?"

"I don't remember. It doesn't matter. She picked it out for me and it's special."

"You hate mice."

"That's true. Okay, you can throw this one away. Wait! No, don't!"

"What about these red-and-green potholders that are so old and scorched they burn your hands whenever you use them?"

"No. Marge from church made those for me. They were a wedding present!"

"*Fine.* What about this ugly-ass Santa?"

"Jen! *You* gave me that!"

"Was I drunk when I bought it? I apologize for giving that to you. Please throw it away."

Last year when we were packing up, I finally convinced her to throw away about twenty items from her menagerie. It was like an episode of *Intervention* meets *Hoarders*, because my daughter (the future hoarder) was there that day for my mother's intervention and she took well over half of the cast-offs for *her* Christmas decoration collection! So now *I* have to buy a bin for that shit, too!

OVERACHIEVING ELF
ON THE SHELF MOMMIES

By now we have all heard of the adorable little Elf on the Shelf. Almost everyone I know has one. Some people even have two! I was feeling guilty for not having two—apparently when my kids are adults, they'll each want one from their childhood. Ugh. I wasn't looking forward to telling the Hubs why we needed to buy another Elf. Luckily, I didn't have to have that conversation, because a generous reader sent me a second one to round out my collection.

The Elf is a handy little thing to have. The little bastard keeps my children in check this time of year. When there is even a *hint* of rebellion, all I have to do is say "Elf" and my kids snap back in line.

If he's so good, Jen, then why did you call him a bastard? you ask. I called him a bastard because even though my children think he's magic, *I'm* the one doing all the "magic," and I totally suck at it. I forget to move him all the time, and when I forget I have to spin even *more* lies than usual. ("No, Santa can't give you the four-hundred-dollar Lego Death Star. Even though he *says* he makes everything, he can't make Legos and he has to actually go and buy them, and he can't spend that much money on you" or "Well, I don't know why he gave it to your friend last year for Christmas. I bet his mommy and daddy paid Santa to do that, and we don't pay Santa." Thanks a lot, asshole parents who gave their kid the Death Star from Santa! As parents, let's all make a pact that any gift over two hundred dollars comes from Grandma and Grandpa rather than Santa, okay? It would make my life a lot easier.)

But back to our Elf. Our Elf has been a lazy SOB this year. He usually makes his first appearance Thanksgiving night (I get him out when I'm on my way out at 3:00 A.M. for Black Friday). This year we left town and I forgot. He waited until we came back and then he was ready to join our family. Since then he's only gone away four, maybe five times. I am always forgetting to move him. And it should not be difficult. I am literally moving him from the top shelf in my kitchen to the bottom shelf and back again. I'm such a loser that I can't even do that right.

I heard some Overachieving Moms talking one day about how they like to make their Elf do "naughty" things. What exactly did that mean? I asked. "Oh, you know, he bakes cookies in the night and leaves a huge mess for me to clean up in the morning." WTF? "Yes, and one time last year he took all the ornaments off our tree! Teeheehee."

Teeheehee? Why in the world would I make my Elf do something like that? *I'm* the one who has to clean up his mess and redecorate my tree! All so my kid could ooh and ahh over the magic of the Elf for about three minutes until the next shiny object caught their eye? I decided these women were insane.

But then I started listening more closely and realized they are not alone. There are entire blogs out there right now dedicated to naughty/fun Elf behavior. I read a blog by a woman named Danielle that really pissed me off. I should have known she'd irritate me when I read her perky-mom-who-loves-to-make-amazing-homemade-memories-with-her-kids-when-she's-not-secretly-downing-Valium-and-vodka-so-she-can-be-so-damn-perky-and-fun title for her blog. (In case you haven't guessed, I'm proudly unmedicated, and I have the mood swings to prove it.)

This site has 101 fun ideas to do with your Elf. *One hundred and one.* As a friend pointed out, there are only twenty-five days until Christmas—why 101?

I wanted to punch her as soon as I read her top two:

1. Have a marshmallow fight (marshmallows everywhere).
2. Have a pillow fight (feathers everywhere).

Okay, seriously? Does she have a clue how much a down pillow costs? The hell I'm going to destroy one just so I can sweep it up in the morning!

Or like I have the time, desire, or resources to make a red carpet entrance for a doll, as she suggested. I can barely get him out of the box and prop him up on the shelf. We haven't even read the book yet this year and she wants me to literally roll out a red carpet for him. When does she do laundry? When does she work? And most important, when does she sleep?

20. Make faces on school pictures with a marker.

I lecture my children constantly on appropriate materials to write on with markers. A photograph is not one of those things.

It would take years to undo that damage if I did that. I'd have mustaches on every photograph in my home. "The Elf did it!"

24. Read a book.

Yeah, I tried that one on my own the other day (didn't even need Danielle's help to come up with that one). The Hubs didn't see him on the couch reading and he sat on him. The kids couldn't find him because he wasn't on his usual shelf. So much for trying to think outside the box . . . uh, shelf.

32. Switch clothes from one closet to another.

And I do this when? At 4:00 A.M. when everyone is asleep and I'm hauling dresses and jeans from one room to another? And we're assuming my children would even *notice* I did this.

42. Take picture of child sleeping.

This is one I would do just to scare the snot out of them. I'd like to perch the Elf right on their sleeping heads and take a picture of that. I could probably whip that picture out in the summer when they're being bad and it would scare them enough to knock it off. I'll bookmark that one.

44. Knit a scarf or hat.

When I'm not trashing my house with feathers or flour or drawing on the walls, I'll whip up a handmade hat, psycho.

64. Learn multiplication facts.

Huh? Just set him on the table with flash cards? I guess I could do that, but it sounds just as boring as my shelf.

80. Elf packs school lunches but mixes up everyone's lunches. (Each child receives sibling's lunch—great conversation piece at dinner.)

Or source of meltdown at school—you pick.

93. Sit on toilet *outside* on front lawn—if you happen to have an extra toilet being stored.

WTF? Who has an "extra" toilet they can put in the yard? Either she's grasping at straws to get to 101 or she's white trash.

He's called the Elf on the Shelf, not the Elf Who Skydives, Takes Bubble Baths, and Shaves the Dog! Leave him on the shelf so the rest of us slackers don't look so bad. I think I'm just going to lay my Elf on his shelf, tape wires and hoses to him, and tell my kids he's in a coma and hopefully he'll recover before Christmas. That should give me some flexibility.

HO-HO-HORRENDOUS

I *love* Christmas lights. In fact, our whole family loves Christmas lights. We love to drive around and look at them. We love the displays that are set to music and you have to park and watch them flash and dance to the beat. We love the crazy, over-the-top houses with icicle lights on the first floor, blinking multicolored lights on the second floor, blue lights on the garage doors, and the chimney outlined in red. We love when just the peaks of the house are outlined with lights. We love the trees lit up with lights. We love those blow-up Santas and snow globes. It's the cheapest entertainment for us. We have our favorites and we drive by them multiple times in the season—although recently one of our favorite houses decided it was too expensive to run its music and light show, and I've heard that another favorite display has a glitch this year. It won't matter, though; we'll find some other houses to look at. It seems like this year there are more lights than ever. Did I mention I just love them? Because I do.

When I say I love Christmas lights, what I really mean is I love *everyone else's* Christmas lights. I hate putting up our own lights. No one will ever drive by my house and have someone in the backseat beg for a second pass because "it was just so pretty!" Hell will freeze over first.

A Christmas lights spectacular just won't happen at our house because the Hubs is the cheapest guy I know. He would never pay for someone to hang lights on our house. I actually checked into it one year. It costs three hundred and seventy-five dollars. And don't even mention the electric bill. If he was somehow possessed to actually shell out the money to pay someone to hang the lights, then he'd never turn them on because he'd bitch about how much it cost to light them up. We might get an hour of light each night. So not worth the fight for that.

He's also not very brave. He would never climb up to the top of our house to hang the lights himself. Really, though, I probably wouldn't let him climb up there if he wanted to, because it could only go one of two ways:

1. He falls, but he doesn't die. Him dying would be too easy on me. Instead he just ends up paralyzed for life and can't speak. He can only spell out words by blinking at me. He would blame me for making him climb up there to save a measly three hundred and seventy-five bucks and then I'd have to put one of those little sleeping masks on him, because I wouldn't be able to take his blinking accusations any longer.

2. He only gets it half done. He'd do one peak or outline half the garage with lights or something like that and then say, "Yeah, that looks pretty good. You don't need the whole roof outlined. It's fine like that. No one will notice."

Instead, we have two little bushes in the front of our house that we wrap with lights.

This year for some reason I just could not get into the decorating mode. Not that I'm *ever* in the mood to decorate for Christmas, but some years it's more fun than others. There was one year where I just had too much personal stuff that I took on and I really didn't want to make time to decorate for Christmas. It was overwhelming me, and I just decided, *Screw it. I only need to put up one tree for my kids and hang the stockings and, of course, don't forget that Elf.*

We finally found a day to decorate and I told the Hubs I just wanted the "little tree" that year. That's the six-footer that we trekked out to Target for years ago when my mother was coming to town. This tree has all my meaningful and keepsake ornaments on it. It's the "family tree," as opposed to my "show tree." The show tree is such a pain in the ass. It can literally take three hours to get that sucker assembled and lit and I just didn't want to hear the Hubs bitch about it since it's he who has to do it. He was shocked I wasn't going all out this year, but he didn't complain for a second.

He hauled my bins out of the basement, I put up the tree in a day, and we were done.

It was cold that day and neither one of us wanted to freeze our asses off to do the little bit of lights outside. We decided we'd forgo it that year.

Honestly, who was going to care? Like I said before, no one drives by our house and thinks, "Ooh, pretty." We are on the end of a cul-de-sac surrounded by homes that would make the Griswolds jealous. I was very content to be the dark house. So was the Hubs.

Or so I thought.

We came home one night and saw that *everyone* on our street had lights up and blazing. It looked like a landing strip for the airport. Even the new neighbors across the street had lit up their house. In years prior their house had sat empty, and before that a Jewish family lived there, so we hadn't had lights over there since we moved into our house.

The new neighbors were late to the party, but they threw down the gauntlet. They lit every bush, every tree, and around the door, and they even had some light-up reindeer out there. It was actually very tasteful and it looked beautiful.

The Hubs wheeled into our street and came to a screeching halt when he saw their display. "Son of a bitch! They put up lights."

"Yup. Ooh, they're pretty. Go around the loop again so I can see them better," I said.

"Now *we* have to put up lights," the Hubs whined.

"What? No way. It's too cold. That ship has sailed. We're perfectly happy being the dark house."

"No. No. It's too much. Now *everyone* has lights, Jen. We can't be the only ones. What will the neighbors think?"

What will the neighbors think?

Are you kidding me with this shit, Hubs? This is the same man who called our neighbor's two-year-old child a "liar" when he claimed to be four.

The neighbor had looked at the Hubs like he was an idiot. "He was just teasing," the child's father said.

"Nope," the Hubs had said to his face. "He's a liar."

This is the same man who goes to the neighborhood pool and wears full snorkeling gear—including fins—while he swims in five feet of water. With his huge face mask and snorkel he can float around the pool for a long time. He looks like a perv checking out all the *ladiez* underwater.

This is the same man who pulls into the garage and immediately puts the door down for fear someone might actually want to have a neighborly conversation with him. If there are neighbors out in their yards, he puts the door down even faster, practically gassing us to death because the car isn't even turned off yet.

"What will the neighbors think?" I asked. "Probably not much. It's not like we've ever done a full-on laser light show set to Mannheim Steamroller. I think they'll just think what they always do. That we're assholes. A couple of lights in the bushes isn't going to make a difference."

"Yes it will. We've got to put the lights up. Tomorrow."

And that is how I found myself outside the next day flinging a few half-dead strings of lights haphazardly through our frozen bushes. We stopped after two bushes because our hands were numb and we decided it was as good as it was going to get.

I stepped back to admire my handiwork and realized I must really love this guy, because it looked ho-ho-horrendous.

ONE MAN'S JUNK IS MY PRECIOUS CHILDREN'S GIFT

Every year my extended family gets together at Uncle Olaf and Aunt Ruby's house to celebrate Christmas Eve. We end up staying up very late, eating way too many sweets, and playing games. Now, most families play Monopoly or charades on Christmas Eve, but not my family. Remember, I told you, I come from a long line of overachievers. Overachievers wouldn't be satisfied playing the same games everyone else plays. Heaven forbid!

Even though Uncle Olaf isn't related to me by blood, Aunt Ruby chose well. Uncle Olaf has been forced to learn and adapt to keep up with the bar that my aunt sets. So every Christmas Eve we play a game that Uncle Olaf has made up for our entertainment just for that evening. That's right. We never play that game again. It's a new game every single year. It's usually a family-based trivia game. Meaning that if you don't know my family well, then you're never going to win. That being said, it's pretty much rigged for my grandmother to win. Even the in-laws who have been around for forty years can't answer some of Uncle Olaf's questions, because who really knows the name of my mom's third-grade teacher? Or how much (to the ounce)

Aunt Ruby weighed at her birth? Uncle Olaf is no dummy. He doesn't want to be cut out of the will.

Just so the new spouses of the cousins don't feel like complete idiots, Uncle Olaf always includes something easy for them. Like how many children Jenni and the Hubs currently have—and bonus points if you can name them. They're never going to win, but he doesn't want them to hate his game.

The best questions are the video trivia challenge ones. Uncle Olaf will show you an extreme close-up of an eyeball on his big-screen television. He'll give you a clue: "This eyeball belongs to someone in our family." You get one guess and then he zooms out and you can see the owner of the eye. It could be himself as a baby from his own baby picture, one of my kids from their school pictures, or his daughter's dog. You just never know whom Uncle Olaf considers "family." It's very rare that anyone gets these questions right. They're way too hard. Most people can't even recognize their own freckled nose. I keep hoping that one of these years he'll feature scars from everyone's gallbladder surgery or appendectomy, but whenever I mention this as a possible idea, I'm told that I'm weird. He's showing us pictures of dog's eyes and calling them family and I'm the weird one?

Back to the story now. If you get the answer right, then you get to choose a white-elephant gift from the pile under the Christmas tree. Everyone brings several crappy gifts. We all compete to see who can bring the worst stuff. Throughout the year we all hit garage sales, clearance racks, and Freecycle to see what we can find. There are a lot of gingerbread-scented candles and singing reindeer. Very rarely is there anything good that you actually want. Some of the same gifts turn up year after year to be regifted, like the beautifully framed eight-by-ten head shot of Uncle Olaf, the one-thousand-piece panoramic puzzle depicting the Last Supper, or the matching strawberry-flavored edible underwear the Hubs and I received as a wedding gift from my grandparents. Well, really they were from Uncle Carl; he just taped Grandma's card to the box as a joke. I thought it was hilarious. Grandma did not. Now that I think about it, I haven't seen the edible underwear in a few years. I think my cousin Zelda received them last. I'm sure she took them out of circulation because they upset Grandma each time she saw them and my kids were starting to ask how underwear could be edible. Either that or she's a fan of strawberry.

Last year the rules were a little different. Along with your white-elephant gift you also had to—oops, I mean *got* to—pick one or two of my grandmother's extra Christmas ornaments to keep. My grandma is getting older and has moved into a retirement community. She had to downsize and give away a lot of her belongings. She and her children went through her stuff and picked out the Christmas decorations she wanted to take with her to her new home and left the rest behind for her kids to sift through. After they chose what they wanted, the remainders ended up in the slush pile that the rest of us got to dig through on Christmas Eve.

We were all cracking jokes about the quality and condition of these poor misfit ornaments. There was an obvious reason Grandma and her kids didn't want them: they were horrible. Everyone kept "forgetting" to pick an ornament or two and had to be reminded constantly.

When the night was over and Grandma had handily won the game, it was time to head home. Before we left, Gomer and Adolpha asked if they could have another of Grandma's keepsake ornaments (they are really the only ones in our family who have any sentimentality, plus they're tiny hoarders and they can't pass up free shit). I could see that there were several left, so I told them it shouldn't be a problem. I helped them dig through the box to find something that wasn't too hideous—like the angel made from a corn husk or the dingy needlepoint Santa. And then all of a sudden I saw something that made my heart stop. Buried deep under all of the unwanted, shabby, broken, old, and decrepit ornaments were two tiny treasures. Two little wooden ornaments that *my* precious snowflakes, Gomer and Adolpha, had made for their great-grandparents six years ago. (I know, because I always write the date on the ah-may-zing and adorable works of art that they foist on relatives.) Gomer had been a beautiful little three-year-old boy when he carefully painted the ornament. Sure, he mixed all of the colors together and ended up with black, but still. It was gorgeous. Truly one of a kind. My sweet, angelic Adolpha had been barely one when she haphazardly slapped a bit of red paint on her masterpiece.

"Grandma!" I shrieked. "How could you?"

"What?" she asked, clearly confused.

I held up the ornaments to show her. "My children—your great-grandchildren—made these works of art for you! And you just tossed them in the junk pile? Like trash?"

"They're not trash! Those ornaments are heirlooms! You're supposed to take them to remember me by when I'm gone."

"These heirlooms are crap, Grandma. You didn't want them. No one wants them. Whatever is left after tonight will be thrown out. You think my kids' ornaments are crap." I was really irritated. Sometimes I think my kids and I are at the bottom of the totem pole in this family. She'd never throw out shit from my cousins' kids.

When Grandma realized why I was pissed, she looked for an

out. "Not me! It wasn't me. I would never. It was your aunt Ruby!"

"Me?" Aunt Ruby cried. "What did I do?"

Grandma continued, "Yes! Aunt Ruby was the one who helped me choose what to take to my new apartment and what to give away. In fact, she must have put those in the box when I wasn't looking."

Aunt Ruby came closer to see the ornaments in question. "Oh. Those," she said, shaking her head. "Mom, we agreed that you shouldn't take them with you."

"You agreed with her, Grandma?" Gomer asked, his eyes big.

Aunt Ruby tried to smooth things over. "Now, Jenni, you must understand. Grandma couldn't take these with her. We had to pick and choose. All of Grandma's ornaments *match* now."

"Oh, they match now? Well, I'm *sooo* sorry to hear that my little children's ornaments were too ugly for her tree!"

The room was silent. Everyone could tell that I was upset, and no one was quite sure what to do to make it better. I looked like I might burn down someone's Christmas tree, and my kids looked like they might burst into tears. Grandma and Aunt Ruby gave each other a knowing look, and then Grandma said, "Actually, now that I think about it, it was Uncle Filbert's fault!"

Uncle Filbert. Hmm. He was a bit of a curmudgeon, but would he really throw out my toddlers' handmade Christmas ornaments? I looked around to confront him and remembered he wasn't there. Uncle Filbert was spending Christmas in Mexico that year.

"I remember now. He was the one who went through the ornaments. I'm sure he did it. So you see, Aunt Ruby and I had nothing to do with this!"

My eyes narrowed. I wasn't sure I was buying what she was selling. How convenient for Grandma and Aunt Ruby to throw Uncle Filbert under the bus. The one uncle who wasn't there to defend himself.

"Well, he has a lot of explaining to do when he gets back in town. You better believe I'll be asking about this," I said.

"Mommy," Adolpha asked, "can we take our ornaments home and put them on our tree?"

"Of course we can," I said, gathering them up.

"No, I want them," said one of my cousins.

"No. Give them to me," said another.

"Wait!" Aunt Ruby cried out. "I would like them. I have a place of honor for them." She plucked the kids' ornaments from my hands and proceeded to hang them on the front (not tucked in the back) of her "good" tree. Her tree where everything is gorgeous and perfect. At first I didn't want her to keep them, but I could tell it was killing her to leave the ornaments hanging from her beautiful boughs. I knew she was trying to make things better with me, but I wanted her to suffer a little bit, because I knew that Uncle Filbert had had nothing to do with the decision to throw out my kids' gifts. Of course it was her. Uncle Filbert has never cared if a Christmas tree's ornaments "matched."

What I didn't expect was how much it bothered my little Overachieving Mom-in-training to see those hideous ornaments tucked in the perfection that is Aunt Ruby's good tree. As soon as Aunt Ruby hung the ornaments on the tree, Adolpha said, "Ewww, Aunt Ruby, those *do not* look good there. It's ruining the tree. I would take them off. The tree looked better without them."

And just like that, my daughter went to the dark side.

WAIT. WHO IS THE REASON FOR THE SEASON?

Our family goes to church every Sunday. Really. We do. The Hubs is the son of a preacher, so every weekend he drags our butts out of bed and makes us go to church. If it were up to me, I would probably read a book and let the kids sleep in most Sundays, but the Hubs won't hear of it. He's single-handedly trying to save our souls. It's probably a good thing. If you've read this far, then you know my soul could use some saving.

When the kids were little I really liked going to church, because they would go to the nursery and I'd get an hour to myself. Now that they're older, they go to Sunday school. This is okay, I guess. Except for the part where I have to deprogram them.

See, I know what I believe, but what I believe isn't the "official" word that most believe. I'm different from a lot of the Christians I'm surrounded by. I'm not a big fire-and-brimstone type. Also, I'm the sort of a believer who thinks God loves everyone: Jews, Muslims, little children, gays, douchebags, believers in the theory of evolution, you name it. Sunday school tends to teach my kids stuff like "Of course there were dinosaurs on Noah's ark, Adolpha, because the world is only two thousand years old!" or "Yes, Gomer, your friend Ahmed is going to hell. You need to battle him for his eternal soul before it's too late."

I've been so busy deprogramming the kids of all this nonsense that I always assumed they were learning the basics. Or so I thought.

It was the Christmas when Gomer was eight and Adolpha was six. The kids and I were decorating their Christmas trees. As I've said before, I'm not really into Christmas decorating, but my mother is and she's passed that overachieving gene on to my children. Over the years they've collected ornaments for their trees from the clearance bins after Christmas and my mom's cast-offs. Enough that they have their own personal bins full of decorations just for the Christmas trees they put up in their rooms. I was in Adolpha's room helping her hang yet one more pink poodle ornament on her little tree when I heard Gomer yell from his room across the hall, "Mom! Can I put out my nativity?"

"Yes, go ahead," I replied. Both kids have their own plush nativity sets that they can display in their rooms. They received them when they were babies and they like to arrange them every year.

"Where's mine?" six-year-old Adolpha asked. "I want to put mine out, too."

"Look in your closet," I said, digging through a box of Eiffel Tower ornaments. What? You don't have an "Ooh La La, Paris"–themed tree in your house?

"Hey, Mom!" Gomer yelled again. "I can't find my baby!"

I couldn't understand what he was talking about. "What baby?" I called back. "I'm helping Adolpha. If you need me, come to her room, please."

Gomer stomped into Adolpha's room holding his Joseph and Mary dolls. "I said I can't find my baby. I've only got these guys."

"These 'guys' are Mary and Joseph. They're kind of important people in the nativity," I said. I could hear Adolpha digging in her closet, and each crash of something falling to the floor only made me more exasperated.

"Okay, whatever. I can only find Mary and Joseph. Not the baby."

There was another loud crash from Adolpha's closet. I needed to investigate now. It sounded like a whole rack of clothes had fallen down. "Well, I don't know what to tell you, Gomer. It was all there last year when we put it away. Go look again."

Gomer ran from the room and returned a few seconds later. "I've only got the basket. It's empty. I can't find the baby." Gomer showed me his empty manger.

"Keep looking, Gomer. He's got to be around somewhere." I left him while I went to check on Adolpha and the mess in her closet. It was as I had suspected: she'd pulled down an entire rack of dresses on herself.

I was helping her hang up her clothes when Gomer returned several minutes later. He was victorious. "I found him! I found my baby!" he shouted. "I found my baby Moses!"

"Uh-huh," I mumbled from beneath a pile of Hello Kitty crap.

"Come on, Moses, let's get you in your basket," Gomer cooed.

"Wait, Gomer," I said, finally ignoring Adolpha's mess and giving him my full attention. "*Who* did you say you found?"

"Baby Moses."

Are you kidding me, Sunday school teachers? You've spent so much time focusing all of your efforts on converting new followers to Christ or distributing coupons for chicken sandwiches at

God-fearing businesses that I think you forgot to teach my kids some of the key players. Namely, *the* key player.

"Gomer, that isn't baby Moses," I said.

"Sure it is," Gomer insisted. "Moses was the baby in the basket. This is a basket." He held up the manger.

"Yes, Moses was a baby in a basket, but that's not a basket. That's a manger," I said, waiting for the lightbulb to pop on over his head. I got nothing from him.

"What's a manger?" he asked.

"I don't know. Like a trough."

"A what?"

"A thing used to feed animals. Only they put baby Jesus in there like a crib. *Away in a manger*," I sang, thinking surely that would jog his memory.

"Why would they put a baby where animals eat?" Gomer asked.

"Remember, there was no room at the inn, so Mary and Joseph went to the stable and Mary gave birth there."

"That doesn't sound like a good place for a baby at all. She should have been at a hospital."

"Gomer! This was biblical times. There were no hospitals."

"Really? Where were babies born, then?"

Ugh. I did not want to get into this conversation right now. "Listen, it doesn't matter where the other babies were born. Jesus was born in a stable and then he slept in a manger."

He looked at me and shrugged. "Well, this isn't a manger. This is a basket. Moses was a baby in a basket."

I tried one more time. "Gomer. What holiday is coming up? What are we decorating for?"

"Christmas!" he answered quickly.

"Right. And what is Christmas about?" I asked.

"Presents!" yelled Adolpha from her closet.

"No!" I said, shaking my head. "No. We celebrate a birthday. Whose birthday are we celebrating? He was born in a stable . . . a long time ago . . ."

"Grandpa?" Adolpha called.

"No! What's wrong with you two? Mary was his mother and Joseph was his father . . ."

Gomer looked at me with a blank expression.

"Gomer," I tried again. "The very first Christmas was the birth of our savior. He is also known as . . ."

He looked at the doll in his hand. "Uhhh . . ."

I gave up. "That's baby *Jesus*, Gomer!"

"Who?" Gomer asked.

"Baby Jesus."

"Wait. Jesus was *there*? At the first Christmas?" Gomer asked.

"Uh, *yeah*! Of course he was. *He* was the baby. We celebrate his birth at Christmas! Come on! You know that! Right?"

"Ohhh . . . ," Gomer said, finally understanding. "Whoops. I just always thought this was baby Moses," he said, looking at the baby in his hand.

Adolpha emerged from her closet with her nativity clutched in her hands. "Hey, look! I found my Jesus," she said, holding up Joseph.

I need to speak with their Sunday school teachers.

HOW SHOPPING WITH ME AT CHRISTMASTIME IS THE BEST BIRTH CONTROL THERE IS

A few years ago I found out that two of my cousins have a tradition where they go out to dinner and then go Christmas shopping with our grandma. I had no clue this was happening until my grandma let it slip during Thanksgiving dinner at my house. "Why don't you ever come shopping with the girls and me?" she asked between bites of pumpkin pie.

"What do you mean, Grandma?" I asked, trying not to retch at the disgusting smell of pumpkin.

"Your cousins and I go shopping for their Christmas presents," she said, polishing off her pie.

I looked across the table at my cousins. One stared guiltily at the ceiling, and the other had an emergency text message she needed to send out right that moment. "I didn't realize you three went shopping together," I said.

"Uh, y'know, it's no big deal," my cousin Lucille said, putting down her phone. "We just go to dinner and do a little shopping is all."

"Why wasn't I ever invited?" I asked.

"We started it a while ago," my cousin Eloise said. "You were really busy."

"Doing what?"

"I think we started doing it right after Gomer was born. We didn't want to bother you and make you feel like you had to come," said Lucille.

My cousins are childless and husbandless. They think escaping from my house requires a nail file and a smoke grenade. They're kind of right, actually.

"You never even invited me."

"You girls never invited her?" Grandma asked. "I had no idea. I just assumed you didn't want to come, Jenni."

"Well, sometimes it can be hard to get away because of the kids, but they're older now. It wouldn't be hard now. I think I'd like to come with you."

"Wonderful," Grandma said. "Now, let's all pick a date that works."

We got out our calendars and started comparing dates.

"December first?" I asked.

"I can't," replied Eloise. "I have a work event that night. What about the eighth?"

"I can't," Lucille said. "It's a Tuesday. That's my date night with Rodney."

"How about the ninth?" I asked.

"I have to be in court with my clients that night," Eloise said. "I'm looking at my calendar and really all I have is the eighth or the fifteenth."

"That's still date night," Lucille said with a shrug.

Date night. How cute. I remember having date night back in the day. Now date night is a stroll through Target while my parents keep my kids. "Could you miss date night that week?" I asked Lucille. "Eloise can't miss court."

"I'll see what Rodney says," Lucille said.

"Never mind," Eloise sighed. "I'll skip the work party if you can do the first."

"I can do that one," said Lucille.

"Great. Then it's settled," I said. "How does this work?"

"We'll meet at the mall at six on the first. Grandma takes us to dinner and then we shop," said Lucille.

"Fine. I'll see you there."

A few weeks later I found myself shopping with my twenty-something cousins and my eighty-something grandma.

"Now, Jenni," Grandma reminded me, "each grandchild gets one hundred dollars to spend. You need to spend yours on your whole family, so you each get twenty-five. These girls each have a hundred to spend on themselves, so don't be jealous that they're getting nicer things. It's the only way I can do it."

"It's okay, Grandma. I understand. But my family isn't here and I just might spend the whole hundred on myself." I enjoy teasing my grandma. It drives her crazy.

"You should!" said Eloise.

"I wouldn't like that at all, Jenni," said Grandma.

"Don't worry. I'm just teasing."

I wasn't sure what I was going to buy. My kids wanted toys, but that would have to wait for another day, because I couldn't imagine Eloise and Lucille hanging out in Toys "R" Us with me. The Hubs never wants anything, so I could spend his money on myself, but I wasn't sure what I wanted. I thought I'd see what my cousins were buying; maybe it would give me some ideas.

Eloise is a young, single lawyer with a nice paycheck and expensive taste. She had her eye on a Michael Kors bag. Now,

Grandma's money was never going to buy her a Michael Kors bag, but she thought she'd put it toward the bag and use her own money for the balance. We went to the department store to get a closer look at the purses.

"It's beautiful," I said, touching the soft leather.

"Would you ever carry it?" she asked.

"When I was your age and had a real job I totally would have."

"You don't think it's outrageous to spend this much on a purse?" She showed me the price tag. It was as much as the car payment on my minivan.

"Not at all," I replied. "You have the money. You have places to carry this bag. Where would I take it? The playground? A PTA meeting? Maybe someday I'll carry purses that nice again."

"You used to carry nice purses," Grandma said. "I remember."

"Yeah, I did. And then I traded in my purse for a diaper bag."

"When was the last time you had a new purse?" Grandma asked.

"I don't know. A while. I was going to get a new one last year, but then Gomer needed a backpack for school and the one he wanted was close to a hundred dollars. He carries it every day and I rarely leave the house, so it made more sense to spend the money on him."

"I see," said Grandma. "I understand. I have four children, Jenni. You have to be careful with your money and budget it." She patted my hand and walked away to check on Lucille.

"I think Grandma will freak out when she sees how much it costs," Eloise said.

"Nah, she's oblivious. She's got a stack of cash in her purse. Just ask for the money and then I'll distract her while you pay. She'll never know how much it cost."

"What about Lucille?"

Lucille was young and single, too, but she was a teacher and didn't have nearly as much disposable income as Eloise had. "I can distract her, too. She wants jewelry. I'll take her and Grandma to that department while you check out."

"Thanks," Eloise said.

After Grandma gave Eloise her cash I asked Lucille to show me what she had her eye on, and we headed over to the jewelry department.

"I like this necklace," Lucille said, pointing to the case.

"It's pretty," I said.

"You should get a necklace, Jenni," Grandma said. "I never see you wear jewelry."

"I know. I used to wear it before Adolpha came along, but she ripped off every necklace I owned. She's seven now, but I still don't trust her."

Grandma nodded sadly and took Lucille's necklace to the checkout.

"Adolpha has more jewelry than you," said Lucille.

"Yeah, she does, doesn't she?" I said, shrugging. "She also has a better wardrobe than me. But she's the one who leaves the house every day, so . . ."

"You keep saying that a lot," said Eloise, coming up behind me, swinging her new bag.

"Saying what?"

"That your kids should get the good stuff because they leave the house more than you. Now that you've had kids and you're writing all the time you barely—"

"Shower?" Lucille asked. "Comb her hair?"

"Buy yourself something you really want," Eloise said.

"That's not true," I said. "I can buy anything I want. I just want practical things now, that's all. For Christmas, the Hubs and I are getting each other a front-loader washer and dryer. It's like a dream come true."

"What do you mean? That's what the Hubs is getting you for Christmas?" Eloise asked, frowning. "That sounds awful."

"No, not at all. It's wonderful. I've been wanting a set for years now. It will cut my laundry time literally in half. No joke."

"So you'll have nothing to open on Christmas morning?" Lucille asked.

"Nope."

"Surely he'll get you something. Anything. A charm bracelet or a new sweater?" Lucille asked. I could tell the thought of having nothing to open on Christmas Day was extremely upsetting to her.

"No, nothing, Lucille. Do you know what a pair of front-loaders costs? Believe me, I'll be lucky if I get a birthday present in a few months."

"What is with your husband? Didn't you get a vacuum for Mother's Day?" Eloise asked me.

"I did! I got the Dyson. I was so excited when I saw the box."

"You were excited for a vacuum?" Lucille asked.

"Do you know what the Dyson can do? Have you seen what my couch looks like after my kids have eaten a box of crackers while binge-watching Disney propaganda?"

"Well, now I'm officially depressed and never getting married," said Eloise.

"I thought I wanted kids, but now I'm not so sure," said Lucille.

"You guys, don't feel bad for me. My life is great. I have my bad-ass minivan, yoga pants for every day of the week, and a husband who is willing to buy front-loaders as his Christmas present. Not many husbands would do that."

I was puzzled. Neither of them looked the least bit envious.

"Uh-huh," said Lucille.

"That's it. We're going to find you something that you really want tonight, Jen," said Eloise.

"I told you. There's nothing."

"I don't believe you. Think hard. There must be something," she said. "I'll even chip in if it's more than the twenty-five bucks you get from Grandma—which, by the way, is a total rip-off."

"I know!" said Lucille. "What's up with that? You get married and all of a sudden your present budget is cut by seventy-five percent?"

"You guys, she has to. It's that way with my parents, too. Most of the budget goes to the kids now. It's fine."

"That's terrible," said Eloise. "Inexcusable, really. We have got to get you something amazing tonight."

"Yes!" said Lucille. "Let's get you something nice!"

I have to admit, I was getting excited. It had been a long time since I'd really shopped for myself. I looked around the department store and took it all in.

The first area I saw was the shoe department. Did I need any new shoes? I only wear flats, tennis shoes, and Crocs. All of the high heels on display looked wonderful . . . and painful. Nope. No shoes.

Next was accessories. I gave up the diaper bag a few years ago and was back to carrying my outlet mall Coach bag. It held everything I needed—wallet, phone, glasses, lip gloss, Handi Wipes, toothbrush, gum, Matchbox car, Silly Putty, bubbles, easy-reader book, Band-Aids, juice pouch, corkscrew, hairbands (man, I'm so glad I don't carry a diaper bag anymore!)—and still looked good. A new purse would be fun, but nothing really appealed to me.

Then, out of the corner of my eye, I saw something. It was like a glimmer or a sparkle that caught my eye. What was that? It winked and flashed in the bright overhead lights.

"What's that?" I asked, following the light, my cousins close behind me.

It was a rhinestone on a leopard-print slipper. "Hello, gorgeous," I said, picking up the slipper.

"Those aren't shoes, Jen. They're slippers," said Eloise.

"I know. I spend a lot of time in my office in the basement and the floors are hardwood, so they're cold on my bare feet. I haven't had a new pair of slippers since before Gomer was born."

"You're going to get slippers?" Lucille asked.

"Leopard-print slippers?" Eloise asked.

The leopard print had caught my eye, but then I saw the Isotoners with memory foam were on sale. "Isotoner," I whispered. "The good stuff."

"What did you find, Jenni?" Grandma joined us.

"Slippers," sneered Lucille. "She wants slippers."

"I want slippers, Grandma," I said, grinning from ear to ear. "The ones with memory foam. I've wanted them for a long time, but I just couldn't justify spending that much money on slippers."

"They're on sale, Jenni. You have some money left over. Do you see anything else that you like?" Grandma asked.

I looked around, not expecting to see anything else. And then I saw the greatest creation known to womankind. "That is amazeballs," I said, picking up a fuzzy thingamajig.

"Oh God. What is that?" Eloise asked, laughing.

"It's like a blanket that goes over your head," said Lucille, wrinkling her nose.

"You guys. It's a fleece hooded muumuu. My three favorite

things: fleece, hoods, and muumuus. And look, it's on clearance. Why would this ever be on clearance? It's the most beautiful thing I've ever seen. Grandma, I want this, too, please."

My cousins died a little inside that night and vowed to never age past thirty. But little do they know. Forty is when you can get away with wearing a fleece caftan and no one even bats an eye. I'm warm and cozy (because unlike that POS Snuggie, this sucker covers your back and has a hood—genius!), plus it comes in cool, fun, hip designs. Mine is black and white polka dots because black is slimming, even in a one-size-fits-all fleece blanket with armholes.

SOMETIMES IT'S HARD TO TELL THE DIFFERENCE BETWEEN A HOME INVASION AND AN OVERZEALOUS CREW OF CHRISTMAS CAROLERS

What is the deal with Christmas caroling? Who are these people who enjoy this sort of behavior? I thought Christmas caroling went out of fashion when Dickens died, but I've been told that I'm wrong. For some reason my house doesn't attract too many Christmas carolers. I'm thinking it has something to do with our less-than-festive light display. Or it could just be the Hubs. Hard to say.

It was about eight-thirty on a cold December night when our doorbell rang. "What the . . . ?" the Hubs grumbled, hitting pause on the DVR. "Are you expecting anyone?"

"No, of course not," I said, motioning to my fleece muumuu, which by the way is the best Christmas present I've ever received. (Thank you, Grandma!) "I would have at least put on yoga pants if I knew someone was coming over."

"Hmm. Let's just ignore it and see if they go away," the Hubs said.

We started up the DVR again, and about a minute later the bell sounded for a second time. "Oh come on!" I said. "If that's the neighbor kid ding-dong-ditching us again, I'm going to be pissed. They wake up the kids every time they do it."

"I don't think it's them. They only do it in the summer. It's too cold tonight to be assholes."

"Well, then who is ringing our doorbell? It's way too late for the UPS guy."

"Shh," the Hubs commanded. "Listen. What is that?"

I strained my ears, and then I heard it: the low hum of a group of people whispering on my porch. "Go check it out," I whispered. We crept to the front door so we could peek through the window. *Is this a home invasion?* I worried. I'd recently seen a story on the news where people would ring a doorbell, and if no one answered, they'd kick in the door and steal the Christmas presents from under the tree—like the Grinch, but with a gun. "I think we're being robbed," I whispered, grabbing my cell phone.

"Is the alarm set?" the Hubs asked.

"Yup," I replied, snatching the closest weapon I could find: a Black and Decker Dustbuster that I'd told Gomer to put away earlier that day. Which he of course didn't. The Dustbuster wasn't that lethal, but I was confident I could whack someone upside the head pretty good with it. It would have to do in a pinch. I've never actually punched anyone in the throat, but I was fully prepared to go all Mama Bear and jab an intruder in the throat with that Dustbuster. I'm a little bit like a ninja with my cleaning tools. I don't just stop dust bunnies, I stop attackers.

The voices outside were getting louder, and the bell rang again, causing me to jump. The Hubs pulled back the blind and looked out the window.

"Who is it?" I asked, dialing 911, my thumb poised over the send button on my cell phone.

"Oh shit," the Hubs said, visibly relaxing. "It's only carolers."

"It's who?" I asked.

"Christmas carolers."

"Oh man!" I complained, dropping the Dustbuster. "They scared the shit out of me!"

"I know," the Hubs said. "I was a little nervous, too."

"Crap. Now what are we supposed to do?"

"I have no idea."

"Do we know any of them?"

"I'm not sure," the Hubs said.

"Here, let me look," I said. "Maybe we could pretend we're not home." We traded places, and when I looked through the window, I accidentally made eye contact with a woman I recognized from church. She waved vigorously and pointed me out to her fellow singers. "Damn it! She saw me."

"Who did?"

"What's-her-face from church. The greeter who always says hi to us and asks us if we're new, even though we've been going there for five years. She saw me. Now she knows we're home."

"What now? I guess we should open the door?"

"Not yet. I don't even have a bra on," I said. I opened the blinds and held up one finger—the universal sign for "one minute"—to the church lady. I ran into the bedroom, flung off my fleece muumuu, and grabbed my bra, grumbling the whole time. "It's like ten degrees out there! Who goes out singing on a night like tonight?"

"I don't know. Should we invite them in to sing?" the Hubs asked.

"No! They'll wake the kids," I said. "Plus our house is a mess. I can't have that woman see what a disaster we live in."

"I don't even think they'll notice the mess," the Hubs said.

"We have luggage from our trip to New York in June sitting in the front hall because you won't put it away."

"We're going to need it again in a few months when we go to Florida for spring break!"

"Fine. Whatever. I'm not going to argue about the suitcases right now. Let's just go out there and listen to one song and then send them on their way," I said, pulling my shirt back on and slipping into some shoes.

"Okay," the Hubs agreed.

We opened the door and were met with an arctic blast of air.

"Merry Christmas!" the church lady said.

"It's awfully cold to be out singing tonight, isn't it?" I asked, my teeth chattering.

"The spirit of the season is keeping us warm," said a man near the back of the group.

Uh-huh.

"Jen, close the door," the Hubs griped. "You're letting out all of the heat!"

"Aren't you coming out?" I whispered.

"No. It's too cold. I can hear them sing through the door," he said, closing the door in my face.

Are you kidding me, Hubs? You asshole. I stood on the porch shivering. I wondered if I could ask for another minute while I grabbed a coat. It wouldn't even take a minute since I never hang it up—it's always thrown over a dining room chair right inside the door. *Eh, screw it. Let's not waste any more time,* I thought. I just wanted to get this over with. "Okay," I said. "Hit it!"

Someone pulled out a pitch pipe and gave the group a note. I don't think anyone heard the note, because they all started on a different one. I was assaulted with the worst version of "We Wish You a Merry Christmas" my poor ears have ever heard.

Now I was met with a huge dilemma. I felt stupid standing there listening to my own private (terrible) concert. I've never been good at that sort of thing. I have no idea what to do with myself. Should I smile and nod? Tap my foot? I knew the words; should I join in and sing along? I wouldn't sound any worse than their warbling. I still hadn't decided what to do when I realized they were wrapping up. *Oh good, but what now?* I wondered. *What should I do when they finish? Clap? Demand an encore?* This is why I should never answer the door after December 1 unless someone has made an appointment.

I went with clapping. It seemed like the right thing to do. "Thank you very much," I said. "That was nice." I turned to go back inside the house.

"Hold on! We're just getting started!" the church lady said.

"Uhhh . . ." *Just getting started?* My feet were numb! "It's so cold! I can't believe you want to keep going!" I exclaimed. "You really don't need to keep singing. I'm good. Surely there are other homes you want to visit?" I asked, motioning to all of the dark houses on the cul-de-sac. My street is never that dark. The jerks must have heard the off-key singing and hit the kill switches on their lights.

"Doesn't look like many are home. We can wait while you get a coat," the church lady said.

Shoot. What could I say? *I'm too cold to stand here and listen to you sing another off-key song* didn't seem very neighborly or Christmasy. I sighed heavily. I was going to have to get my coat and listen to some more songs. "Hang on one sec," I said. "Let me get a coat. I'll be right back."

I opened the door and looked back at the group. "Can I get you guys anything?" I asked stupidly. There were at least twenty people on my front lawn. What was I offering? Hot cocoa for everyone? A glass of wine? All I had in my kitchen was water and a gallon of milk that had expired the day before.

Luckily no one took me up on my offer.

I ducked back in the house to grab my coat. The lights in the front hall were all off and the Hubs was back in our bedroom, snuggled into the warm bed. "What are you doing?" I asked him.

"I got cold," he said. "Did you lock the door?"

"No. They want to keep singing. They have more songs."

"You're kidding."

"No."

"So then what are you doing here?"

"I'm getting my coat. I was freezing out there. You need to come out with me. It's super awkward. I don't know what to do with my hands or where to look. Am I supposed to tip them? Do you have any cash? And I'm saying stupid stuff. I asked them if I could get them anything!"

"What? Like a hot toddy or something?"

"I guess so. I feel like they're freezing off their asses on my porch bringing me fucking holiday cheer, so the least I could do is offer them a nip of something!"

"We don't have anything except water and expired milk, Jen! Did anyone say yes?"

"No. Thank goodness."

"It's okay—someone else probably gave them drinks. They've got to be drunk, right? Only drunk people would go caroling."

"I don't think so. They seem really with it for drunk people. Plus, there's a bunch of kids with them. *They* can't be drunk."

"You gotta get back out there. They're waiting for you!" the Hubs said.

"You should come, too. *Pleeeeeease*," I begged. "Don't make me go alone."

"No way. I didn't want to open the door, but you let the church lady see you. You should have been stealthy like me. Now you need to go out there and listen to them."

I yanked on my jacket and stomped out of the bedroom.

I opened the front door, hoping they'd given up on me and had moved on to the next house. No such luck. I listened to the group sing three more songs: "Away in a Manger," "O Little Town of Bethlehem," and a jaunty rendition of "Santa Claus Is Coming to Town." At that point, I felt like I'd done my duty—I'd smiled and clapped and lied to them about how wonderful they sounded. I was trying to think of a way to graciously go back in my warm house and send them on their merry way. I hadn't signed up for this. They had. I was ready to put my muumuu back on and cuddle up to watch *The Walking Dead*.

They were just about to start singing another song when the porch lights went off abruptly. Then the pathetic Christmas lights on the bushes in front of the house were extinguished, plunging us into darkness. We stood there in stunned silence. I couldn't believe the Hubs had turned out all the lights. Well, that's not true—I could totally believe it, but I was still a little shocked. No. No, I wasn't. I shrugged and was about to apologize when the front door swung open and the Hubs stepped out on the porch and announced, "Show's over, folks. This is private property and you need to get a move on now."

And that's why after that night, carolers always skip our house.

YOU CAN KEEP YOUR COOKIES, I'M JUST HERE FOR THE BOOZE

I hate cookie exchanges more than you can know. I realize that as soon as I write this, I will never be invited to another cookie exchange, and I'm really okay with that. Let's face it, I only go for the booze.

These stupid gatherings are just another way for women to compete with one another over who can make the most adorable, delicious, *ah-may-zing* bullshit cookie on the planet. There are usually stupid awards like "Best Presentation," "Most Festive," "Tastiest Cookie," and my favorite, "Best Packaging." "Best Packaging"? It never even crossed my mind to "package" my cookies! I wouldn't even know where to begin. Maybe I'm supposed to wrap them in parchment paper and tie them with baker's twine or something stupid like that. The Christmas season is one of the busiest and most stressful times of the year, and I don't have time to bake cookies that will be judged. I'm judged enough—I'd rather not go *looking* for it.

When you read about the benefits of a cookie exchange, magazine editors love to throw around the idea that cookie exchanges are "time savers." The assumption is that everyone is going to be baking several dozen cookies during the weeks leading up to Christmas anyway, so you might as well bake several dozen of all the same kind and then just trade them for someone else's signature cookie. I don't know about you, but the only time I *ever* bake several dozen cookies is when I'm invited to a cookie exchange, so really it's the cookie exchange that creates a ridiculous amount of work.

I also have an issue with the sanitary conditions the other partygoers' cookies are prepared under. I am not a real dog lover. I also don't care much for cats. Both dogs and cats tend to shed everywhere, and nothing makes me retch like finding any kind of hair in my cookie, but for some reason an animal one is even worse. Even the thought makes me shudder.

You can always tell which animal lover baker is going to have a hair in her cookie. She's the one who walks in the door already covered in cat hair. I make a mental note of her Tupperware and stay as far away as I can from her hairy Yuletide offerings.

And then there is the fact that I don't like cookie exchanges because I'm a picky cookie eater. To look at me you'd never guess this is true. I look like someone who has enjoyed a cookie . . . or six . . . in my time. But I feel very strongly about what cookies I choose to ingest. For instance, if a cookie doesn't have chocolate as a main ingredient, then what is the point? Why even bother making a cookie without chocolate? I also don't like coconut in my cookies, and there is something about a cookie exchange competition that makes the ladies bust out the coconut. I can't stand sugar cookies. I think this overwhelming distaste goes back to my chocolate issue, but it also goes along with my desire for variety. There are almost always at least two or three different sugar cookie offerings. You can't just cut those suckers into different seasonal shapes and call that original. Plus, they're usually covered in some sort of festive sprinkles that I will find on my kitchen floor for days, because my kids eat like small farm animals. If I had my choice, though, I guess I'd choose a sugar cookie any day over something with almonds. Yuck.

I hate the pressure of walking around the table laden with cookies and taking some of each. I don't want a macaroon or someone's dried-out hockey puck. In my opinion, biscotti aren't cookies, they're doorstops, and while gingerbread smells delicious, it doesn't make the cut because it's not chocolate. Honestly, it's a waste for me to take any of these cookies. They will just get thrown out since no one in my house will eat them.

I feel like everyone is watching me while I try not to turn my nose up at their offerings. There's always that one pushy broad who wants you to take hers, even though you've passed it by. Twice. "Try the biscotti, Jen! I think you'll love them!"

I plaster on a fake smile and say, "I'm allergic to biscotti."

"I didn't know that was possible."

I shrug. "Yeah, it's a new allergy. I'm having one of those medical alert bracelets made. It's a real problem. I can't have biscotti, gingerbread, or sugar cookies. I also can't have anything made in a home with cats. Were these chocolate mint brownies made by a cat owner?"

The hostess stops dumping booze into the cider and speaks up. "I made those, Jen. We just have fish."

"Perfect! I'll take double of those since I'm leaving the biscotti."

I despise the pre-planning that goes into attending a cookie exchange. The invitation informs me I must bring six dozen cookies to trade, two dozen cookies to share with the party-goers, and a container to take home my picks. So that's three containers to hold a total of eight dozen cookies. I don't have that kind of storage capacity. I am expected to have something pretty and jolly and preferably sparkly to display my two dozen shareables on so that they look beautiful on the hostess' goody table. I don't have that kind of shit. I usually arrange my offerings on a paper plate festooned with holly or some sort of winter wonderland shit that was left over from a school party. Then I need a large container (it would be nice if this was a holiday-inspired piece as well) for the six dozen cookies that I'm trading. And finally I need an empty third container to bring home the six dozen cookies I pick up. But before any of this, I must type up and print out (on cheery fucking paper, of course) copies of my recipe for everyone to take home and shove in a drawer. *Son of a bitch!* That is a lot of work, and I'm not sure I'm cut out for that.

Instead, I'd rather go and drink the hostess' spiked cider and eat a couple of chocolate cookies from the nosh table while I laugh with the girls. I'd like to bring my two dozen crappy (chocolate) cookies to share (or mostly eat myself, whatever) and leave with nothing except a full belly.

When I do get invited to a cookie exchange, here is my go-to recipe. If you make this one, the only award you'll win is the Martha Stewart Just Died a Little Inside Award.

(I bet you never thought in a million years you'd find a recipe in my book, did you? Yeah, me neither, but my mom insists that I have at least one recipe in here if I want to call this a holiday book. So, here you go, Mom!)

Festive Pretzel M&M Bites

50 pretzels (preferably the Christmas-shaped ones, but I
    won't judge you if they're not, but they can't be rod-
    shaped, as that will ruin this recipe)
50 plain or peanut Christmas M&Ms (I prefer peanut)
50 Hershey's Kisses

Preheat oven to 400°.
Line up pretzels on a baking sheet with an unwrapped
    Hershey's Kiss in the middle of each pretzel.
Place in the oven for 2 minutes.
Remove and *quickly* press an M&M into the center of the
    softened Kiss.
Let cool and serve on holly-festooned paper plate from the
    Dollar Store.

SUBURBAN MOMS' ENDLESS CHRISTMAS CONVERSATION LOOP

It's three weeks before Christmas and the malls are swarming with people trying to buy something fairly cheap—but not too crappy—for all of the inconsequential people in their lives.

You can always find a horde of women fighting over a bin of clearance scarves they can give to their hairdressers, manicurists, kids' teachers, and piano instructors. Lucky for me I don't feel the pressure to give my hairdresser anything for the holidays. I just don't book any appointments between late November and early January. It's hell on my roots but easy on my wallet. I have so little experience with manicures that I had to ask my mom what she calls the lady who does her nails. My kids' teachers always get a Target gift card from us, and we don't have a piano teacher, because being forced to take piano lessons as a child has scarred me so deeply that even if my kids begged to take piano lessons I'm not sure I'd give the instructor a gift.

Because I have so few people to buy for, I can hang out in the hat department and try on the hottest new styles in headwear while I eavesdrop on a couple of Overachieving Moms digging through the scarves. It's like the scene from *Lady and the Tramp* where they follow the same piece of spaghetti to each other's lips, only it's separate ends of the same scarf they're tugging on. And they're not in love, so they're ready to throw down with whoever is on the other end . . . until they realize it's their very best frenemy.

There's a formula to these conversations. It's always the same endless loop with a few changes depending upon the time of year.

Kori: Hey, Whit! Great minds think alike, huh? What are you doing here?

Whit: Oh! Kori, it's you. Hi. I'm looking for something for my cleaning lady. This scarf would be perfect for Florence. What about you?

Kori: When I dropped off Cavanaugh at school this morning, Mrs. Jenkins was complaining how cold it is on the playground, so I thought I'd get her a scarf.

Jillian: Mrs. Jenkins, huh? I've hated her ever since she told Kinslee that cheerleading wasn't a sport. I have eighty-two trophies in my home that prove otherwise! I'd probably let that bitch freeze.

Kori: Jillian! You're so bad!

Whit: Hey, Jillian, you're here, too, huh?

Jillian: Of course I am here. Where else am I going to get Ms. Landers a decent gift? My real problem is Mr. Gregson. What do you get a male teacher? Pink really isn't his color, and only the women's scarves are on clearance, of course.

Whit: I saw mugs with mustaches on them over there. According to my stylist, anything with mustaches is hot this season.

Kori: You're so good, Whit! I would have never thought of that.

Whit: You have to keep up with the trends and styles, Kori. It's not that hard.

Now that the gifts for the unimportant in their lives have been decided, the conversation moves into the I'm-so-tired humblebrag zone. This is where all of them must compete against one another to see who is *literally* the busiest and the most exhausted. In order to win the title of Most Overscheduled, you can't just have a calendar full of shopping dates and hair appointments. That simply won't do. Workouts must be doubled, because it's cookie season. Parties are a huge drain on these ladies—both throwing them and attending them. A good overachiever is double- and triple-booked most weekends. Typically whoever is planning an exotic trip over the holiday break wins this competition, because besides the double workouts and the copious amounts of invitations they must accept or decline, there is also the packing and other obstacles that must be overcome: passports need to be renewed, the dog needs to be boarded somewhere and the usual place is full, and a bikini wax must be endured.

Jillian: Great idea, Whit. I don't want to have to go to another store. I'm *sooooo* busy. I am *literally* falling asleep on my feet. Is anyone else exhausted?

Kori: Tell me about it! You wouldn't believe my to-do list if I showed it to you. It is *literally* a mile long.

Whit: I would believe it, because mine is *twice* as long. I guarantee it. *Literally* no one is as far behind as I am this season.

Jillian: Only twenty-two more shopping days! I don't know how we're supposed to get everything done!

Whit: I know what you mean! It's not just the shopping. I have so many parties I've been invited to! I will have to skip some of them. I just can't attend them all. It's impossible. And, honestly, I don't *want* to attend them all. Are either of you going to Leila's caroling thing?

Jillian: No way. I was freezing last year and only three people opened their doors.

Kori: It was kind of fun last year, except I had to pee so bad the entire time, I could barely sing.

Jillian: Well, even if I wanted to, I couldn't go. We'll be in Mexico.

Kori: How fun!

Jillian: If you say so. I think it will be fun once we get there and I can sit on a beach with a margarita. But it's been unbearable what I have to do before we leave. I have to pack and find someone to take the kids' hamsters—any chance either of you would want a hamster for the break?

Whit: No way.

Jillian: I still need to get my eyebrows threaded and a pedicure. I need to call my insurance provider to make sure we're covered internationally. I have to stop the paper and the mail. There's so much more that needs to be done, but the worst part is our flight leaves at 6:00 A.M. I'm already dreading the 3:00 A.M. alarm clock.

Ding, ding, ding! We have a winner!

Whit: Well, I don't envy you all of that nonsense, but at least I think we're agreed that we can take Leila's event off the calendar. That's a start, but that still leaves so many others.

Kori: The parties are the worst, Whit! And it's not just us! Luna has four Christmas parties to go to just this weekend and she wants a new dress for each one.

Jillian: I don't blame her. I would, too.

Kori: Yeah, but she's eight. She can't repeat an outfit?

Whit: Maybe if the parties are held in *your* neighborhood.

Jillian: Are you still living in Ainsley Lake Ghetto?

Kori: Yes, the parties are being hosted by our Ainsley Lake *Meadow* neighbors.

Whit: Then yeah, you can repeat Luna's outfits.

Jillian: Otherwise no.

They've always got to get a neighborhood smackdown in there somewhere. The queen bee needs to let the wannabe know *literally* where she ranks. They quickly move on to helpful advice that actually sucks. All these women think that everyone's lives could be easier and more simplified if they'd just implement "systems." Typically, these systems have a thousand steps for something that should be two steps.

Whit: I wish shopping for dresses was the only thing I could complain about.

Jillian: Shopping is so low on my list. I need to make a plan of attack for all the wrapping I need to do.

Whit: Oh, that's easy. I have a system for wrapping.

Kori: I need to get my wrapping under control. What's your system, Whit?

Whit: Well, I took the number of gifts I've purchased for everyone and I divided that number by twenty-four, and so now I know I need to wrap thirty-two gifts per day in order to get it all done in time.

Kori: Did you factor in the ones that need to be shipped and hostess gifts for parties?

Whit: Of course, Kori. That's part of my system. Once I made my list of gifts I prioritized them by when I need them. For instance, I need Florence's gift and the nanny's gift by the twenty-fourth, but I need teacher gifts by the fifteenth, so the teacher gifts go into an earlier batch of wrapping. Anything that needs to be shipped is done the first week and sent out immediately so there is less clutter in my wrapping area.

Kori: Genius.

Jillian: How do you keep it straight? Is there an app for that?

Whit: No. It's not that hard. I simply make a spreadsheet and then I mark off the gift as I get it wrapped. I also cross-reference the current list with the previous years' lists to make certain that I'm not duplicating gifts or forgetting anyone. It's also a lifesaver if everyone has their own wrapping paper.

Kori: What do you mean?

Whit: Well, for instance, all of the hostess gifts for a cookie exchange. They're all the same gift: a cookie sheet and Christmas-tree-shaped spatula. I wrap them in the same wrapping paper. I put them all under the formal tree in the foyer and then I know that on my way out the door to a cookie exchange, I need to grab one of the gifts wrapped in adorable gingerbread man paper.

Jillian: Oh, I do that, too. Each family member has their own wrapping paper at our house. My daughter's gifts are pink with white snowflakes and my son's are Christmas camo. It makes Christmas morning go so much smoother, too. No one has to try to read my gift tags—they just know which gifts are theirs. Now that I'm selling Pampered Chef, it makes my hostess gift shopping easier. Pizza cutters for everyone! I wrap them in their own paper, too—brown bags from Trader Joe's that I cut up, and then I use baker's twine as ribbon. It's so cute *and* environmentally friendly.

Whit: Exactly. Like tonight. We have a holiday work thing with Brick's co-workers. I know that I need to grab a couple of the gifts in the silver foil paper.

Jillian: You do silver foil for work parties?

Whit: I have to now. Brick's boss was offended last year when I gave him Jesus Is the Reason for the Season wrapping paper. He's Jewish. I guess a few of the others are, too. Brick asked me to try to neutralize this year. I still put red bows on them, though. I hate blue.

Kori: Well, it was a Christmas party. What do they expect?

Whit: His boss calls it a "winter party" and it's so awkward, because you have to keep remembering to say "Happy Holidays" instead of "Merry Christmas."

Kori: So annoying!

Jillian: Brick's boss was offended because you said "Merry Christmas" and gave him a gift with Baby Jesus on the wrapping paper?

Whit: Yup.

Jillian: Ugh. This war-on-Christmas thing has got to stop. *You* should be offended that he's not throwing a Christmas party for the office.

Whit: That's what I said! But this is Brick's boss and I can't have him lose his job over my hurt feelings. I have to be the bigger person.

Kori: You're so strong, Whit.

Jillian: That's true, but it's like religious discrimination.

Whit: I know. But what can we do?

Kori: Well, I love your systems, Whit. I think these are great ideas! I'll try anything to make my life easier this time of year.

Jillian: This year I hired a designer to decorate the house for me. It felt great to take that off my plate, and my house looks *ah-may-zing*. It looks so good I could charge admission. All of my neighbors are totally jealous.

Kori: Oh, I don't know about that. I could never have someone else decorate my house. It's family tradition to decorate together. It's one of our favorite things to do.

Jillian: Well, I think from here on out my family tradition will be to hire Kris Kringle Kreations.

Whit: You should ask them to do your Christmas cards, too, Jillian.

Jillian: Excuse me? What do you mean, Whit?

Whit: Don't be offended or anything, but the quality of your cards has really gone downhill in recent years. Just sayin'.

Ooh, shit just got real. She said "just sayin'." Everyone knows that's the "fuck you" of the suburbs. The holiday tension must really be getting to these ladies. Their passive-aggressive putdowns just jumped to Defcon 1.

Jillian: Is that true, Kori?

Kori: Well, since Whit mentioned it, I'll add my two cents. It's just my opinion, for what it's worth, but it does nothing for me when I receive a cheesy photo card from Costco.

Whit: Don't get me wrong, I like to receive a family photo, but

I like it inside a nice, heavy card, and preferably with a letter attached.

Kori: Oh yes! The letters are the best! I love writing my letter. I work on it all year long. You haven't done a letter in a long time, Jillian.

Jillian: Well, I'm very active on Facebook and Instagram. My friends read all of my status updates. I think it's weird to send out a letter telling my friends and family news they have already read online. That's so boring. I get your letter, Kori, and I'm all, "Yeah, tell me something I don't know."

Whit: Oh yeah? Well, did you know that Kori got Botox?

Kori: Whit!

Jillian: You did, Kori?

Kori: Yes. It was an early Christmas present from Phil.

Whit: Do you think it's strange how much he likes to give you cosmetic procedures as gifts?

Kori: Not at all. I'm glad that he wants me to look my best and that he's willing to spare no expense to help me achieve that.

Jillian: Botox! Of course! That's what is different about you!

Kori: I didn't put it on Facebook. How did you know, Whit?

Whit: Easy. You can't furrow your brow anymore!

Kori: No, I can't. Not at all.

Whit: I'm assuming Phil didn't make you use a Groupon?

Kori: I convinced him that when you're putting a paralyzing poison in your face, you should spring for the good stuff.

Whit: Smart.

Kori: So what do you guys think?

Jillian: It looks really fine. I just would never do it because I'm in sales and I need to be able to move my face. It would look untrustworthy if my forehead were immobilized.

Whit: Yeah, it's good for *you*, Kori. I wouldn't do it myself. I've decided to age gracefully rather than fight it every step of the way with needles and knives. I don't see the need to be so plastic.

Kori: But your boobs are fake, Whit.

Whit: That was done *before* I made my decision not to do any more, Kori. *Now* I'm done.

Kori: Oh.

Jillian: Now see, you should put your Botox news in your Christmas letter.

Kori: No, I can't. But I did write about my obsession with oil pulling. Have you tried it? I have so much more energy! It might be what you need to help you get through your to-do list, Whit.

Ah yes, it wouldn't be a proper suburban mom chat without someone dropping some new fucked-up health thing she's trying now. They've gone fat-free, sugar-free, dairy-free, and wheat-free, and then they adopted the caveman diet—I mean paleo diet. Now they're all pulling oil. They literally stick a glob of solid coconut oil that's the consistency of Crisco in their mouths and swish it through their teeth until it becomes a warm gloppy liquid. They try to do this for twenty minutes without puking. I don't know the science behind it, but I don't care, because there is no way in hell I will ever gargle something that closely resembles a mouthful of jizz.

Whit: Oh, I've been oil pulling for three years. Twenty minutes every day. I don't like to talk about it since it's so trendy now. It's almost embarrassing how many people are doing it. My naturopath told me about it long before it was so popular. Or was it my homeopathic doctor? I can't remember now. Actually, it was my hairdresser.

Kori: Oh. Well, I've only been doing it for a couple of weeks. I'm up to fifteen minutes already.

Jillian: Must be nice. I don't have an extra twenty minutes a day for anything. Especially this time of year. It's hard enough to get ready for my trip plus get my double workouts in and run the kids to all of their extracurricular activities. I guess I could pull oil while I'm waiting for basketball practice or cheerleading or capoeira class to let out!

Kori: Is Truman doing basketball this season? I haven't seen you at any of the games.

Jillian: We moved up to a competitive team.

Of course. You can't get away from a group like this without at least one reminding them all that her child is some sort of athletic prodigy.

Kori: I didn't realize there was competitive basketball for nine-year-olds.

Whit: There's a competitive team for almost any age if you're willing to pay for it.

Jillian: Truman was *invited*. We didn't even know this team existed. Doreen invited us to join.

Whit: Speaking of Doreen, have you made your cookies for her cookie exchange tomorrow night?

Jillian: Of course! Aren't yours done?

Whit: Not quite. I've still got to make them this afternoon.

Kori: Are yours gluten free, Jillian?

Jillian: Definitely. I have a delicious paleo recipe I'm making.

Kori: Mine are gluten free, too. We've been gluten free all year—nothing's going to change for Christmas.

Whit: The cookie exchange was tough for me since I'm off sugar now.

Kori: Oh! That's right. I forgot.

Jillian: How could you forget, Kori? It's all she talks about anymore.

Kori: True.

Whit: I've decided to add natural sugar back into my diet, so I'm bringing fruit kabobs.

Jillian: To a cookie exchange?

Whit: I'm doing Doreen a favor. Last week she answered her door with a cookie in her hand. Who does that? I'll tell you who: people who binge on cookies, that's who.

Jillian: Doreen does look like she's been packing the cookies away, but still, fruit seems like an odd choice. It's the one time of year you can go a little wild with the diet. Surely there's a sugar-free cookie out there?

Whit: None that I like. The fruit kabobs will be a huge hit. I'm making elves' heads with grapes and strawberries. I'm sure they will taste better than your wheat-free and dairy-free hockey pucks.

Jillian: They're not hockey pucks! They're chocolate-covered nut krispy treats that I shape like lumps of coal. It's adorable.

Whit: It's disgusting. Last year I heard someone ask Doreen if they were lumps of poop.

Jillian: What? Are you serious?

Kori: I thought they were reindeer poo. I thought it was a funny idea.

Jillian: That isn't funny, Kori, that's revolting. Only someone gross could find that funny.

Whit: This is just another reason why you need to make a sign that states clearly what your cookie is called. Make sure your lumps of coal are labeled.

Kori: I still think reindeer poo could be funny.

Jillian: Well, I don't! What are you making, Kori?

Kori: I'm making gluten-free pumpkin snickerdoodles. Everyone loves pumpkin.

Whit and Jillian: So true!

Kori: You guys, is that woman staring at us?

Uh-oh. I've been spotted. I quickly grab oversized sunglasses and try to blend in with my surroundings.

Jillian: Which woman?

Kori: The one over there wearing giant sunglasses and a knit hat.

Whit: Oh my God! It's her again.

Jillian: Who?

Whit: The weird pajama woman. Remember, she wore her pajamas to pick up the kids at school and then gave everyone lice?

Kori: I don't think her kids ever had lice.

Whit: Doesn't matter. She's so weird. I feel like she's everywhere we go and always eavesdropping on our conversations.

Jillian: Oh, I know her. She's the one who brings those pretzel things to Doreen's every year and calls them cookies.

Kori: They're delicious.

Whit: They're not cookies.

Jillian: Her house is always half lit for Christmas. I told Kris Kringle Kreations they should call her.

Kori: I heard she's funny. Kenadee's mom told me.

Whit: I highly doubt that.

Jillian: I'm with you, Whit. She looks like the type of person who would find reindeer poo cookies funny.

I would, actually.

I SHOULD HAVE HAD A DAMN HOLIDAY SYSTEM

I used to think there was nothing worse than the mothers who bragged about their "systems." It seemed like no matter where I went (or what conversations I eavesdropped on) I heard moms extolling the virtues of their blessed systems. These moms had systems for everything: before school, after school, meal planning, workouts, extracurricular activities, and so on. In my opinion, systems sounded dumb. Most of the ones that I heard about required a ridiculous amount of setup, and I wasn't convinced there was a lot of savings to be earned in the long run. What I failed to understand is that systems don't save you time. They save your ass.

It was a week before Christmas and I was starting to feel the pressure of the clock ticking in the back of my mind. The Big Day was closing in fast and I still had a lot to do. I wasn't done shopping for our extended family, I needed to bake a shit ton of cookies for cookie exchanges I had no desire to attend, I hadn't written my humblebrag letter, and my bare "Nice Tree—Don't Touch" Christmas tree stood in the living room with bins of ornaments stacked around it. I wasn't worried, though. It's always like that. I just knew that the pressure meant it was time to kick it up a notch and go into what I like to call "scramble mode." Scramble mode is when I start digging out all the presents from my numerous hiding places and assessing what I have. I don't keep track as I'm shopping, because again, I really prefer to do things the hard way. I'm not a fan of hitting the stores in the weeks leading up to Christmas, so I try to buy presents throughout the year as I see them (of course, the Hubs likes this because I tend to buy stuff on clearance). The bad part about buying throughout the year and then stuffing gifts in hiding places around the house is that I forget where I crammed them. I squirrel presents away in various closets, in the attic, in the garage, and in the back room of the basement, and I've occasionally hidden a few under a blanket in the trunk of my car. Then, before I know it, it's a few days before Christmas and I think, *Crap. I need to start wrapping presents or else I'm going to be in trouble.* The problem is, I usually have no idea where half of my loot is located. *Shit. Where did I put them this year? I should have made a treasure map.* So I begin hunting. It's like a scavenger hunt, but without any clues. Sometimes I don't find everything, and that's when Christmas almost gets ruined.

By the time Gomer was seven years old, he was a pro about what he could and could not ask Santa Claus for. He always gave Santa a list to choose from, and that year it was:

1. Nintendo DS
2. Skateboard
3. K'nex roller coaster set

He showed me the list and told me he was fairly certain Santa would say no to the Nintendo DS, because he was already working toward earning one if he got straight A's by the end of the year and Santa would not want to interfere with that arrangement. He also thought Santa would say no to the skateboard, because he won't bring "dangerous" toys. So, assuming he made the Nice List (he's always worried that there's a chance he won't make it), he was confident Santa would bring the K'nex roller coaster.

I agreed with his logic completely and bought the roller coaster about a month before Christmas. I remembered being in Costco and seeing it. I remembered putting it in my cart. I remembered paying for it. I remembered leaving the store. I didn't remember a damn thing after that.

I surrounded myself with the bounty I'd reaped from my nooks and crannies, compiling all my gifts, but it kept bugging me that something was missing. It wasn't until I saw Gomer's list for Santa hanging on the Christmas tree that I realized what it was—the roller coaster! I quickly went from scramble mode to panic mode. There isn't much that will ruin Christmas in my eyes, but my kid not getting something on his Santa list would be extremely fucking traumatic for both him and me.

I went back through all my sneaky spots. I looked in the trunks of our cars. I looked under beds. I even looked through every closet at my mother's house. I could not find the roller coaster anywhere.

I was so frustrated! I knew it was in my house somewhere, but where? Sure, it would turn up over the summer, but that would be too late. I would get out life vests and the bucket of pool toys and I'd find the roller coaster hidden behind them. Or maybe I would find it under the bathroom sink in the guest room. I was positive it was going to be in some random, ridiculous place that would make absolutely no sense. I would find it and the bizarreness of the location would scare me so much that I would seriously wonder if I'd been drunk or high when I hid it.

I didn't have a lot of time, and I was at a complete loss. The next day I went back to Costco to buy another one. Of course, they were sold out. I finally confessed to the Hubs that I'd lost Gomer's Santa gift.

"This is why I wanted to be truthers," he said, exasperated. "*I* wanted to tell them Santa doesn't exist, but *you* insisted on the magic! Santa makes so much damn work for us!"

I don't insist on much magic, but I do think the kids need to get something off their Santa list. I'm not a total asshole.

"Well, what are we going to do?" I asked him.

Just then my mother walked in the front door. She'd taken the kids to see Santa and to get their pictures taken. She'd done this so I could turn the house upside down looking for the roller coaster without any "help" from the kids. We made eye contact and I shook my head slightly: *I didn't find it.*

She sidled up beside me and whispered, "You've got more problems. Adolpha changed her mind. I couldn't hear what she asked Santa for, but I know it wasn't a Bitty Twin."

Adolpha had had one item on her Santa list: a boy American Girl Bitty Twin.

She already had the girl twin, and she really wanted the boy twin so she could pretend they were her and Gomer.

I'd been all ready to buy the twin. *This'll be great,* I'd thought. I'd put the word out to the extended family that American Girl was on the ticket this year, so they bought clothes and accessories for the doll. It was going to be an American Girl Bitty Twin Christmas. But now my mother was in full-on panic mode, because she'd blown her whole budget on a double stroller for those damn overpriced dolls. Shit!

"Let me know how it goes," my mother said as she left. "I'll have to find the receipt."

"Hey, Adolpha," I asked casually, "how was Santa?"

"Good."

"What did you ask him for?"

"He knows what I want."

"Oh, that's right. A Bitty Twin, right?"

Adolpha sort of shrugged.

"Not a Bitty Twin?"

"Adolpha changed her mind, Mom!" Gomer said. "I told her it was too late. I told her we're too close to Christmas and Santa can't switch now."

Such a good boy, that Gomer. He always follows the rules. However . . . "That's right, Gomer. It *is* very difficult for Santa if every kid in the world starts changing her mind a week before Christmas. *However,* it's not impossible. I was looking at your list earlier today, Gomer, and I was thinking it's not too late to change your list if you wanted. Maybe you'd prefer to get a new Lego or something?"

"No way, Mom. I'm not taking any chances. I gave Santa three choices. Any of those will be great. If I start changing my mind a lot and making more work for Santa, he might put me on the Naughty List and not bring me anything!"

The Hubs rolled his eyes at me.

"Santa told me you can change your mind, no problem!" Adolpha yelled. "He said I could change my mind whenever I wanted."

Oh, did he now? Maybe he forgot that I'm the one working all of his magic!

"So you did change your mind then, Adolpha?" I asked.

"Yes. Santa told me to whisper it in his ear and he'd make sure it was under the tree on Christmas morning."

Damn you to hell, stupid mall Santa! What is wrong with you? Every good mall Santa knows he needs to say the gift really loud so that we can hear, too.

"Why don't you whisper it in my ear too? I'd like to know. Remember, I have to approve all Santa gifts. No live animals, nothing dangerous, that sort of thing."

Adolpha sighed heavily and then whispered, "Doggie Doo."

"Doggie Doo?" I asked. "What is that?"

"It's a game! We saw it on television!" exclaimed Gomer.

Of course! Television! The cheapest babysitter in the world if you don't take into account how much shit you have to buy your kids because they saw it in the commercials.

"When I told you I wanted a Bitty Twin you said it was very expensive," said Adolpha. "I don't want Santa to spend so much money. He's not rich like you and Daddy." I could feel the anger radiating off the Hubs' body when she said that. "And then I saw a commercial for Doggie Doo and it's on sale. So I want that instead."

I went to the computer and searched for Doggie Doo. I found a plastic dachshund that eats glowing goop and then shits a neon turd out of a hole in his back end while making farting noises. Adorable. The video made Gomer laugh like a hyena. "Gomer, maybe you should ask Santa for this!" I tried.

"No, Mom. Stop trying to get me in trouble!"

When I saw the price I was torn. On one hand, Doggie Doo cost a third of what the Bitty Twin cost. But on the other hand, Adolpha was going to get so many gifts for that stupid baby, and if she didn't get the doll, her other presents would be a waste.

"Hmm," I said, thinking about the adorable denim overall outfit and the Hawaiian flowered swimming trunks my aunt had just bought for the Bitty Twin. "Well, I guess we'll just have to wait and see what Santa does."

I sent the kids out of the room to play so I could speak to the Hubs.

"We have a problem," I said.

"You mean *you* have a problem," the Hubs replied.

"Come on! I need your help."

"Okay, fine," he sighed. "Just go back to Costco and get another roller coaster. When the first one turns up, we'll return it."

"We can't. They're sold out. Apparently it's the hottest toy of the season and you can't find one now."

"Jen, this is why I hate Santa."

I wasn't in the mood to fight, so I agreed. "Yes, yes, he sucks balls. I get it. However, we need to get Gomer something. I was thinking we could get the Nintendo DS," I said. "I just saw them at Target yesterday. They had tons of them. I could run there tomorrow."

"He's supposed to be earning that with his report card," the Hubs said. "Santa can bring it, but he can't open it until he shows us that he got straight A's. It can sit on his dresser and he can look at it when he's working on his homework."

"God, you're an asshole," I told him. "That is so cruel and depressing. Much like what I imagine your childhood was like. Who does that to a kid?"

The Hubs shrugged, completely unfazed. "I just think that if we give him the DS now, he won't have any incentive to get good grades."

"We could come up with a different incentive," I said.

"No. The DS is working well for him. It's really motivating

him. We might not find anything else that works. I say the DS is off the table."

"Then that only leaves the skateboard," I said sadly. "We'll need to plan for an ER bill, too, when he breaks his arm."

"Wow. Now who's cruel and depressing? You have such little faith in our children's abilities."

"I just know that neither you nor I are known for our grace or our athletic prowess. The kid is going to break something. I'm praying for an arm, because the skull is a bit more significant."

"I'll go and get the skateboard tonight after the kids are in bed," the Hubs said.

"Make sure you get a helmet, a mouth guard, knee pads, elbow pads, and wrist guards, too."

"Would you like me to get a feather pillow we can tape to his ass? You realize this is your fault. If you would keep track of where you hide stuff, we wouldn't even be having this problem. There is a perfectly good toy hidden somewhere in this house."

"I know, I know. I suck at organization. I should have kept a list of presents and hiding places. Don't worry about the money, though. When it turns up I can just return it to Costco. They take back everything."

"It's not the money. It's the hassle of it all. If you'd let me tell them the truth about Santa, we wouldn't be having this conversation."

I stayed silent. I didn't want to say it out loud, but he was right. I should have done myself a favor seven years earlier when Gomer was born and just decided we would never pretend there was a Santa. But back then I'd fought the Hubs. "Nooo," I'd begged him. "I think it will be so much fun to be Santa! One time my mom even hired this guy in a pickup truck to come and see us. He was kind of weird and he picked his nose, but C.B. and I thought it was amazing. I want Gomer to have that kind of magic, too!" Yeah, I should have listened to the Hubs, because Santa and his lies had created so much work and stress for me. Still, there was no way I could let the Hubs know that he was right. "Screw you," I said. "You're hilarious. Okay, so Gomer is solved. Now, what are we going to do about Adolpha?"

"Easy. She gets Doggie Doo. We can order it from Amazon and have it here in two days. Done and done."

"But what about my family?" I asked. "They've all bought her stuff for her Bitty Twin. It will be really weird to get gifts for a toy you don't have."

"Tell them to take them back."

"I can't! It's almost Christmas. And besides, the Doggie Doo costs too little."

"What?"

I don't keep the box totals equal for my kids' presents (that would be *way* too much math for my tired brain). So I might have eight things for Gomer and only six for Adolpha, and then I have to add up how much I spent, because even though I don't keep box totals the same, I do keep the dollar amount equal between the two kids. I know, that's stupid math, too, but to me it's easier stupid math. And it's fairer stupid math. Especially when you have one kid who is smart enough to ask for an eighty-dollar video game and another kid who thinks a new box of crayons is the bomb. I learned this lesson a few years ago when the Hubs' parents took the kids shopping for their Christmas presents. Gomer and the Hubs picked out some freakishly enormous Lego set, and Adolpha got a Barbie doll.

"They're not equal," I said. "Gomer's will be more."

The Hubs didn't see this as a problem at all. "Oh no. This is like the Barbie thing, isn't it? What's the big deal? They each got one gift."

"Yeah, but Adolpha got a five-dollar doll and Gomer got a hundred-dollar Lego set. If your parents were spending a hundred dollars on each kid, you should have helped Adolpha pick out a few more things. Maybe some clothes for Barbie or a car."

"But then she'd have more presents," the Hubs said.

"No, she'd have a hundred dollars' worth of stuff, and so would Gomer."

"I don't see it that way," he replied, shaking his head. "You get one gift. Next time Adolpha needs to just pick something more expensive. Same goes here. Doggie Doo is cheaper."

"Yeah, but she picked two things: Bitty Twin and Doggie Doo. I'm getting the doll. She'll get money from my grandparents and she can use that to buy Doggie Doo."

"Jen, you're going to go to the mall in the Christmas madness to get her a doll she doesn't even want?"

"She wants it; she just doesn't realize it. And she'll really want it once she sees the matching sleeping bags Ida bought for the twins."

"We should just start giving the kids cash," the Hubs sighed.

"You're really trying to kill me, aren't you?" I asked. "Cash is not a gift."

"Cash is king. Can you imagine if we gave our kids a hundred bucks apiece and told them they could spend it on anything? They would lose their minds. Plus, their money would go further, because we could go the day after Christmas and hit all the sales. And the best part? We'd get all the credit, not that fat-ass phony Santa."

"Sometimes I hate you and your tiny Grinchy heart," I said.

"I know," he replied, hugging me. "That's why I'm *not* going to suggest that we all go shopping together tomorrow. You go and get their gifts, Mrs. Claus. Make some magic. But this time leave them in the trunk under a blanket."

"Don't let me forget," I sighed.

"I won't," he said. "My heart might be three sizes too small, but my brain isn't."

Christmas morning Adolpha got her Bitty Twin from Santa and the Hubs and I gave her Doggie Doo. It is truly the most revolting game I've ever played, but at least it's better than Candyland. Santa brought Gomer a skateboard, helmet, elbow pads, knee pads, wrist guards, and a mouth guard. It was June when I found the K'nex roller coaster in the back of the garage buried under a stack of pool towels and shoved behind the Hubs' bicycle, which he never rides. I still have no memory of putting it there.

ANNUAL CHRISTMAS LETTERS: THE ART OF THE HUMBLEBRAG

I am as guilty as the next wannabe Overachieving Mom when it comes to the humblebrag Christmas letter. I can't help it. It's in my genes. My mother always sent out an annual Christmas letter that required people to read between the lines to *really* understand what was going on in our house.

For instance, she'd say things like, *Jenni is a junior in high school this year. We're really enjoying the time she spends with us. We are lucky to have a teenager who likes to hang out with her parents.* What this *really* meant was *Jenni is a complete loser without a single friend. We uprooted her and moved her halfway across the country, and now she hates everyone she comes into contact with and we're paying for the hell that we've caused her. We pray every day that she finds a friend, because we can't believe she actually sits home on her ass with us every Friday night watching* The Golden Girls. *Please, for the love of God, someone take this girl off our hands. We'll pay cash. We'd like to go out some weekend and not feel guilty that we left our teenage daughter at home just so we could enjoy a quiet dinner alone.*

Or my mother would write about my brother, *C.B. is keeping busy with school and his extracurricular activities. He's been in a couple of school plays this year, and he attended a dance.* What this *really* meant was *C.B. is a straight-A student and a junior member of Mensa. Don't worry, though, he's not a geek or anything like that. In fact, C.B. was voted homecoming king this fall and he had the lead in both the school play and the school musical. Oh yeah, I almost forgot—he went to the Junior Olympics with his fencing team. Please don't mention any of this to Jenni, as we try not to compare our kids with each other and this will just make her feel bad about herself. Thanks.*

After years of being a part of my mother's letters, I thought I'd never subject my kids to the same humiliation. That is, until I started receiving one from everyone I know.

Once I saw their letters, I was motivated to write my own. I couldn't let those bitches brag about their hardworking husbands who just made partner or the crazy amount of money they spent on books for their voracious (toddler-aged) readers. I couldn't let all those not-so-subtle mentions of new cars and lake houses slip by without a comment. I joined the fray and started writing the humblebrag Christmas letter that I'm sure everyone mocked.

Actually, I'm giving myself way too much credit. The Hubs and I never had enough to really brag about that would be worthy of a good mocking. Instead, my letters probably just got a small eye roll and were immediately binned. My guess is the only letter that got any attention was the 2002 letter announcing I was finally married. I'm sure my friends said, *Finally! What the hell took her so long? We're on our third kid already. Ohhh, she married a Chinese guy. Do you think it's true what they say about Chinese guys?* (I'll go ahead and answer that one: no, they're not all good at math. The Hubs sucks at math.)

Over the years I've made it my mission in life to read every Christmas letter I can find. I'm not sure why I'm drawn to these letters. It's probably because I'm nosy. I want to know how Uncle Tom's ingrown toenail surgery went in June (preferably with pictures) or what Gomer's former preschool teacher is going to name the new puppy she got for her birthday (also with pictures, because everyone loves to look at a puppy they don't have to clean up after). I also enjoy watching the extremes people will go to in order to humblebrag about nothing. Like the PTA mom who says she was "blessed" to be a room mom this year. No one thinks that's a blessing. I read all the ones my mother sends out (she's not allowed to send them unless she first has everyone in the family sign off on their paragraph). I read all the ones she receives. I read all the ones I receive. And since I've become known as a bit of a Christmas letter aficionado, I have friends who send me some of the gems they receive.

So many of these letters are phony bullshit. The worst ones seem to have some common threads:

Almost always the letter is written in a weird third-person voice. (*Joyce is enjoying bunko.* Yeah, Joyce, we know you wrote this letter.)

The family usually has kids. Let's face it, there isn't much to brag about if you don't have kids.

They live in the suburbs.

Maybe this is just typical of the letters from people around here, but it seems like each letter is sponsored by brands—or at least it should be. Everyone drops brand names into their letters, whether it's a car they bought this year or a handbag they received. It's weird. I hope they're making money from those touts, otherwise they're just assholes.

Mom stays home with all the offspring, but she does a lot more than just laundry and school lunches. She has the "most important job in the world." Just ask her; she'll tell you. She'll also be sure to put in some kind of dig about moms who don't, can't, or won't stay home.

The kids are always winning awards for some dumb shit: *Easton was named Most Sensitive Smile this year by the entire third grade, and our eighth grader, Henley, got first prize in the Tri-State Photo Caption Writing Contest.*

Dad barely gets a mention. He always gets the smallest paragraph—even smaller than the family pet's. It's usually something about working hard and never getting a break. Sometimes we hear about a great golf score he had this year or a BBQ contest he won.

Keeping all of this in mind, I decided to write my own Over-achieving Mom Christmas letter. One that was inspired by all the letters I've sent and received over the years.

December 10, 2011

Dear friends, family, and PTA members,

Merry CHRISTmas and happy New Year! I cannot even begin to believe that this year is over and we are so close to ushering in yet another one!

133

Our wonderful family has been so blessed over the last twelve months! We have been so busy that I'm not even sure where to begin!

Jim received a sizable bonus from his firm in December so he celebrated by taking Claire on a Carnival cruise to Mexico in January! They hadn't been anywhere romantic and exotic since their trip to Italy five months ago. It was long overdue! They took full advantage of several excursions, including a sunrise helicopter ride, scuba diving, swimming with dolphins, and snorkeling. After ten days on the ship together, Jim proposed to Claire again! Lucky for him she said yes, because he had already arranged for the captain to officiate at the renewal of their vows so that they could recommit to each other and their family. It was such an amazing and life-affirming day for us both. Claire wore a Monique Lhuillier dress that she bought on board the ship and Jimmy Choo shoes she had luckily thought to pack. Something old, something new—the sea was Claire's something blue! Jim also had the forethought to hire two photographers to document the occasion. If you follow Claire on Instagram, you can see the photos there. The hashtag is #cheartsj4ever.

The romance continued when Jim gave Claire a Honda Odyssey Touring Elite for Valentine's Day. Claire was a bit surprised, since she'd been dropping hints for jewelry and a newer Escalade for months, but it was as if Jim knew something Claire didn't . . .

You guessed it! Claire is pregnant! In June, they got the joyous news that their family is growing yet again.

After four precious boys, many people are wondering if it will be a girl this time. Jim and Claire have chosen not to find out the sex of the baby until their gender-reveal party in January. One of Claire's closest friends is Macy Lawler of Macy Lawler Events (check her out on Twitter) and she has graciously offered to throw them a gender-reveal party. Surely you remember that Macy was the genius behind the gorgeous Potty Party Claire threw last year for Korbin.

If you're not familiar with what a gender-reveal party is, then keep reading. It's a hot new trend where the sex of the baby is revealed at a party in an amazing and adorably cute way to all the guests (including the parents—yes, Jim and Claire won't know until the big reveal, either).

They have attended so many gender-reveal parties this year, and Claire wanted hers to be special and unique. Jim wanted it to be nothing like any of their friends' parties. So many people simply cut into a pink cake or open a box to find blue balloons inside and call that a party. Thankfully, Macy thought these were terrible ideas, too, and she has some fabulous tricks up her sleeve.

Jim and Claire are inviting three hundred and fifty of their closest friends and family to join them at their favorite beach in Maui. You probably recall this beach from their 1999 letter. This is the beach where Jim proposed (the first time!). If you've forgotten the details, you can just go back and reread the 1999 letter or watch the video that was sent that year (if you didn't save either of those, they're archived on Claire's blog). Macy has chosen a neutral baby-themed luau with hula dancers, fire dancers, and surfing lessons. Finally, at dusk a plane will fly overhead and write "Girl" or "Boy" in the sky while pink or blue fireworks explode. It will be spectacular. Macy has been asked to feature this party in a major magazine. We can't announce yet which one it will be, but let's just say the magazine owner's initials are *M* and *S*. Once it's on newsstands, Claire will tweet about it, so make sure you're following her on Twitter! The hashtag will be #alohablessed-baby.

Although Claire is battling morning sickness every day, she hasn't let that slow her down one bit! She continues to volunteer at school (this year she was named PTA president, she's the room mother for all four boys' classes, and she's organizing the school carnival—the school's biggest fund-raiser); she works tirelessly at the local no-kill dog shelter one day a week, where she grooms and exercises the dogs; she is still taking tennis lessons four days a week with the amazing Alejandro; she attends hot yoga and spin classes twice a week; she is leading a weekly 5:00 A.M. gym boot camp class for pregnant mamas; and she started a couples wine club for the neighborhood just before she found out she was pregnant. Whoops! Don't worry, she is sipping club soda now!

Claire has also made a pledge for our family to eat healthier this year. She has started a vegetable garden and she buys only organic and locally produced food. The boys enjoy composting, and Jim built some rain barrels to help water the garden. You can find all of Claire's healthy recipes on Pinterest. You can also find Jim's instructions for building rain barrels there, too. The hashtag is #homesteadingishot.

Our boys continue to astound us on a daily basis. Kelton is a strapping fourth grader now and almost as tall as Claire. He has shown that he is a strong contender on the baseball field. He is on three competitive teams this year. All three teams won national championships. It was a little confusing figuring out *which* national championship is more important, but Kelton knows they're all rare and amazing feats. Kelton is so busy with baseball he barely has time for homework! Please don't get Claire started on his teacher and how much free time she must assume Kelton has to do homework. She obviously does not have children or else she'd understand how busy kids are these days. She sends such a ridiculous amount of work home we wonder what she's actually teaching him at school!

Claire and Jim have heard from a number of coaches that Kelton has what it takes to go all the way but that he needs more time to cultivate his gift. When they took a closer look, Jim realized that only school was holding Kelton back from his full potential. Claire is seriously considering homeschooling him so that he can focus on baseball. All the information she's found indicates that Kelton only needs three hours a day of schooling. But he's so bright, it could probably be lowered to an hour and a half. That would free up so much of his time for training.

Kiran is the most popular boy in second grade. He receives an invitation for a birthday party, a playdate, or a get-together every weekend! Claire needs a separate schedule just to keep up with him and his social engagements. She doesn't know anyone who has as many friends as Kiran. For example, just last weekend Kiran juggled five birthday parties in two days. He was exhausted, but he had a wonderful time. Even though it was a busy weekend, he would not have dreamed of missing out on any of those parties. He knows how much it means to his friends to have him there celebrating with them. Kiran found out this week that he has won the schoolwide award for "Kindest Eyes" and he will be featured in the yearbook and probably the local paper, too, since Jim let them know about his award.

Boys aren't supposed to be called "beautiful," but Kiran is

stunning—inside and out. He stops traffic wherever he goes, and he has such a gentle and loving soul. After some prodding from friends and family, Claire finally hired an agent to pitch the ideas she and Kiran have developed for a television show. His acting coach thought that a series that showcased his acting and singing abilities would be the perfect fit for him. His agent is working on getting a meeting with a company that can't be mentioned, but let's just say it starts with a *D* and features a mouse. In the meantime, Jim started a YouTube channel for Kiran where you can hear him sing. Please check it out, but a word of warning: be prepared to stay awhile. Kiran has the voice of an angel. You won't be able to leave his site!

Kalem is a loving kindergartener. Even though he is only five years old, he is showing enormous promise in art. His art teacher told Claire she should consider hiring an artist for private lessons for Kalem since his love of art cannot be satiated with just one hour a week in her studio at the school. His teacher offered her services, but she confessed to us that she thinks Kalem is beyond her abilities at this point.

You will recall from last year's letter that Claire was considering having Korbin's IQ tested. Well, she did it. She met with quite a bit of resistance, since Korbin was only three years old at the time. Claire was relentless, though, because she was certain Korbin was gifted. Mothers, can't we always tell when there is something unique about our children? Claire wouldn't back down and he was finally tested. The results were inconclusive, but only because the test wasn't designed for a three-year-old to take. All that is known is that he didn't fail it. Claire realized that Korbin needed to be enrolled in school as soon as possible. After careful consideration,

Claire and Jim chose a rigorous French immersion program that is about thirty miles from their home. The commute isn't ideal, but if this school is the best school for Korbin, then it's worth it.

Even though Korbin is only three years old, he was accepted into this competitive preschool program a year early. They don't usually accept anyone under the age of four, but Claire requested a meeting with the headmistress to help educate her as to why Korbin would be a perfect fit for her school. Once she met Korbin she was convinced her *école* needed him.

After only four months, Korbin has already mastered almost everything they expected him to know by May. There is talk of moving him up to the next level. Jim worries about that, though, because it will put so much more pressure on little Korbin. However, Claire feels we can't deny our child a better education, especially when he is practically demanding it. He has proven to us that he is an exemplary student and his talents are being wasted in level *un*.

So many of you have complained to Claire about the pain of deciding what's best for your remedial students, but she wouldn't wish on you the kinds of decisions she's had to make about Korbin. A gifted child is as difficult, if not more difficult, than a remedial or even average one. Be thankful you don't have this kind of stress to deal with. Please pray for the family during this important time of decision making.

While Jim was away on a business trip this summer, the boys convinced Claire to bring home a dog from the shelter where she volunteers. Sparky is the sweetest yellow Lab you'll ever meet. He's wonderful with the boys, and he's a great guard dog for when Jim is traveling for weeks at time. The most unusual thing about Sparky is that he only has three legs. No one is sure what exactly happened to him, since he was brought to the shelter in that condition. Claire and the boys have imagined a fantastic story (with illustrations by Kalem) about Sparky, and they published it on Amazon. It's called *The Totally True Travels of Tripod the Three-Legged Dog*.

Jim continues to work tirelessly at the firm so that he can provide for the family. Claire is so grateful that he insists she stay home with the kids. She can't imagine why any mother wouldn't want to be home with her children. It's such an amazing and rewarding opportunity. Jim agrees and repeatedly tells her that *she* has the most important job, not him. He's been traveling so much this year that Claire teases him he has another family somewhere! So many of you are struggling with the loss of jobs and homes in foreclosure this year. When we hear these stories, our family is so thankful that Jim has always been a hard worker and has always made clear and sound financial choices for us.

Jim's big news this year is that he won our neighborhood "Best Yard" contest three months in a row. When he does get some downtime he can usually be found at the club playing a round (or two) of golf or having fun with his new favorite app, Snapchat. He's always talking to his friends on there!

Merry Christmas and happy New Year!

Much love,
Claire, Jim, Kelton, Kiran, Kalem, Korbin, and Baby K

As I have already confessed, I usually write a holiday letter telling everyone about the fun and interesting things we did that year. *(We had a baby! We had another baby on the same day two years later! We're working a lot! Sometimes we travel!)*

For a few years when my kids were toddlers I wasn't in the mood to write a letter. I was tired and I didn't feel like I had much to say. We hadn't had another baby; yeah, we were still working a lot, but our traveling had really tapered off. It seemed like pretty boring stuff.

But then once the kids got older and I had a bit more free time and they were doing things again that I could brag about, I decided I'd get back into it. Here is the honest humblebrag letter I wrote in 2011 and posted on my blog. (I'm cheap and didn't want to pay to print the letter on cutesy holiday paper, pay for envelopes, and buy stamps, all so everyone can just throw it away as soon as they're done calling me a liar and a bragger.)

December 2011

Dear family, friends, and strangers from the Internet,

Greetings and happy holidays! Wow, I can't believe another year has flown by! What an amazing year this has been!

The kids continue to meet their developmental milestones, and we're real happy about that. Fingers crossed the pattern holds!

The boy is six. He can read now, and he's become a full-fledged grade schooler. I'm not sure what happened to my sweet little boy. He barely gives me hugs and kisses anymore without the promise of a present or the threat of a beating. He continues to be a solid above-average student in all areas except math, where he excels. If you know me personally, you will understand why I am currently having DNA tests done to confirm he's mine, as I can barely add. He's a funny and creative kid who loves to tell jokes and write stories. I'm hoping that he'll be able to figure out a way to parlay these talents into paying the bills, since his father and I still haven't. He started playing soccer this year and is enjoying it immensely. I won't say he's a superstar, but I do think he is a decent player and I believe wholeheartedly that if he keeps at it, he could get a medium-sized scholarship to a midlevel college. Because of his lack of exceptional soccer skills, we're still enforcing our rule that he attend school every day. He's gotta have a backup plan in case he blows out his knee in seventh grade.

Recently Gomer has been shunning clothes. Does anyone else have this problem? The Hubs and I worry that Gomer may grow up one day and discover he's a nudist. We're hoping that as he gets older, he will realize that some activities are simply not appropriate for nude people. Just last week I found him buck naked on the floor of my bedroom practicing his break-dancing ninja moves. "Mom, watch me be a naked ninja break dancer! Ow. Rug burn." That will teach him.

Oh yeah, he learned the *f*-word this week. I'm just glad it was the neighbor kid who taught him instead of me. Ironically, it was the neighbor kid who attends private school because his parents are worried about the evils of public school.

The girl is four. She can write her name and the alphabet now and is ready to graduate from preschool. She's the tallest kid in her class and the tallest kid compared to most children we know. Since I am barely tall enough to drive without a booster seat, DNA tests are being run on her as well. She is bossy, opinionated, and hilarious. (I know where she gets that from: her father.) She's a strong-willed little girl who keeps us on our toes. It's a tough balance to keep her in line while still maintaining her high level of confidence. I'd love for her to still be this kick-ass in middle school. She is a girly girl who loves stuffed dogs, real dogs, skirts, dresses, tights, "cute" knee socks, lip gloss, and high heels. We actually have to have discussions about when it's appropriate to wear lip gloss outside the house (high heels are never permitted). I had to invent a designated "Jeans Day" each week when she must wear jeans, since I bought so many pairs before I knew she was going to be so girly.

Adolpha's big news this year was her broken arm. I have a new appreciation for supermodels who complain about being uncoordinated and gangly at a young age. I get it now. I'm sorry I ever judged you, Tyra Banks. Adolpha is very tall and leggy and she is the clumsiest child I know. We tried ballet last year and she looked a bit like a baby giraffe galumphing among a flock of serene cygnets. After assessing her pros and cons, we decided to enroll her in soccer. We felt her size would be an asset on the field, where she could intimidate and dominate (plus we would only have to focus on one sport between the two kids, so it would be easier for us). Except we forgot: she can't run for shit. She's slow and she spends too much time looking at the flashy accessories the girls on the opposing teams are wearing (wild socks and over-the-top hair bows).

Finally, at a game at the end of the season she focused and got the ball in her possession. She started dribbling the ball down the field and a huge smile spread across her face. She looked up and made eye contact with me as if to say, *You're right, Mom! This is fun!* Just as our little moment passed, her enormous feet tangled with the ball and the herd of bedazzled little girls around her. I watched in slow motion as she fell over the ball and got twisted in a sea of funky socks. I watched her arm bend backward. *Noooooooooo.* She ended up having surgery that night, but she got the best accessory she's ever had: a hot-pink cast.

The Hubs continues to work tirelessly. His drive amazes me. I'm exhausted watching him. He has been making miracles happen for his clients this year, and he loves every minute of it. I made the mistake last year of encouraging him to find some hobbies or fun things to do so he could take a break from work. He found a networking group that he's been spending a lot of time with. Now I'm stuck home with the kids and he's off having fun "networking." Hmm . . . I should have thought that one through a little more. Besides his paying job, he's always got his creative juices flowing. He's got some great ideas and it's only a matter of time before one takes off.

I didn't have a baby this year, but I did give birth to a blog. There have been times it's felt like labor, and it definitely demands my attention in the middle of the night when I have an epiphany that needs to be written down *now*! It's been a great creative (and cathartic) outlet for me to get off my butt and start writing again, and it's inspired me to start writing a book (I'm thinking this letter would make a terrific addition to it). On top of work and blogging, writing, and taking care of my family, I decided I needed more things to do this year because I was bored. So I became the co-leader of a local mothers' organization, I joined the PTA board, and I volunteered to put together an auction for the school (if you have a donation you'd like to send my way, just let me know). Follow me on Twitter, where I tend to send out passive-aggressive tweets during the meetings: *Thx for bringing up stupid pointless question abt major need for pencil sharpeners in cafeteria as we were wrapping up three-hr mtg. #PTAsux*. I only lose sleep between the hours of 4:00 A.M. and 6:00 A.M. worrying about what needs to get done. I am such an idiot sometimes.

We got out of town this year! We took the kids to Disney World for the first time. It wasn't nearly as offensive as I had expected it to be. I'd prepared myself for fifteen-dollar drinks, so when they turned out to be only twelve bucks, I was pleasantly surprised. The crowds were tolerable and I didn't gouge out anyone's eyes waiting on line for It's a Small World. We stayed with my aunt, who spoiled my children rotten. I hope she realizes we can never go back again unless she plans to top herself. We didn't do character meals or stay on the property; I figure we can try that circle of hell next time.

We're getting excited for Christmas around here. This is the first year *both* kids actually want something from Santa. The boy would like a skateboard (not gonna happen unless the skateboard comes with a full-coverage insurance policy for all broken bones) and the girl would like the entire American Girl store.

I don't know if you heard or not, but we have an Elf. He's a real pain in the ass.

Merry Christmas, happy Hanukkah, happy Kwanzaa, merry winter solstice, and any other PC holiday I'm forgetting!

Much love,
Jen, the Hubs, Gomer, and Adolpha

*P.S. Follow me on the blog or find me on Facebook (*People I Want to Punch in the Throat*), Twitter, Pinterest, and Good-*

reads (*I don't have an Instagram account. I have a face for paper, not selfies*) and then you can have a Christmas letter every day in the form of continuous status updates like "Went grocery shopping. Peas were on sale!" or "Swimming at the rec center. Cannonball!" How can you resist?

OTHER HOLIDAYS
(THAT STILL ANNOY ME),
IN NO PARTICULAR ORDER

WHY YOU WON'T BE INVITED TO OUR CHINESE NEW YEAR PARTY THIS YEAR, OR EVER

Years ago, when I first started selling real estate, I took all sorts of classes to learn how to better market myself and my brand. One of the ideas that resonated with me was "throw a party for your clients." I like a good party, and now someone is telling me I can throw a party and call it a business expense? Done and done! A really successful real estate agent was teaching this course. He said that most Realtors throw a Christmas party, but he thought that was a terrible idea. In his opinion the Christmas season is too jam-packed with invitations, and no one wants to give up an actual party with their friends or co-workers to hang out with their Realtor. His advice was to pick a "quirky" holiday, a holiday that no one would normally have plans for. He suggested President's Day or Tax Day.

Say what? Is Tax Day really a holiday? I had no idea what to do for either of these days. Dress up in powdered wigs or give everyone stamps and a ride to the post office before midnight? I'd do better trying to celebrate Arbor Day. At the end of the party I could give everyone a little packet of seeds with a note attached: *I'm a show-er, not a grow-er. Call me for all of your needs!* Get it? I show houses, I'm not a farmer? I'll keep at it, since this line could also work for a professional escort service, I guess.

Anyway, in the hall after the class, I stopped the Realtor who'd taught the class, hoping to pick his brain. I found out that he liked to celebrate Cinco de Mayo with his clients. He's one-eighth Mexican or something, so he felt a connection to that holiday. He serves tacos and nachos and margaritas and has a piñata for the kids that's full of candy and key rings for the future houses you'll purchase with his help. Brilliant!

This got me thinking. I couldn't do Cinco de Mayo. I'm 100 percent European mutt. I probably have some Irish in me, so maybe I could dress up like a leprechaun and tell my clients that a new house is like the pot of gold at the end of a rainbow. I don't really like corned beef and hash or green beer, though.

I'm also a little bit Jewish, but I don't know much about cele-brating Purim except that people like to dress up in costumes. From what I can tell it's a bit like Halloween, but with a religious tone to it. That could be fun, I guess. Until some chick comes as a sexy hamantaschen.

These ideas weren't working. I needed a quirky, offbeat holi-day that people would like to celebrate with their Realtor rather than their family. I needed something that fit with me and my background. And then it came to me: Chinese New Year!

OK, so obviously I'm not Chinese, but the Hubs is and he's my real estate partner, so it kind of makes sense. Also, nobody in Kansas would be too busy on Chinese New Year to come to my house and eat fried rice. It was perfect! I checked the lunar cal-endar and told the Hubs that I wanted to throw a Chinese New Year party every year for our friends, family, and clients.

And oh yeah, I wanted him to cook all the food while I entertained the guests.

Luckily for me, he was totally down with that once I explained the possible return on investment. By now you know how hard it is for me to get the Hubs to cough up a few bucks on party supplies.

The first year we threw the party, I'd only been selling houses for about four months, so I didn't have a huge list of contacts to invite. We invited four couples. We ate at the kitchen table and had a great time. Everyone had bought and/or sold a house that year. That convinced me. I had found my quirky annual holiday.

Over the next ten years we planned a party every Chinese New Year. Each year the guest list grew, because we added all the new clients, plus everyone kept having kids. The Hubs cooked mountains of food, I refilled tons of drinks, our children frolicked in ridiculous silky Chinese outfits, and I forgot to come up with a cute gimmicky giveaway. I should have made fortune cookies with my email address inside or paper fans that opened up to my smiling face and phone number.

The party got so big that we had to extend the hours and make it more like an open house where people could come and go because we didn't have enough room for everyone. The final year we hosted the party, we had more than one hundred people traipse through our home over the course of a day.

That night, the Hubs and I collapsed on the couch and started figuring our ROI on this party. It cost us hundreds of dollars in food and booze, which was negligible when you considered you only need one house sale to pay for the party. It wasn't the actual cost we were figuring; it was more the physical and mental toll it took on us. We looked around our house and found several spots where people had spilled soy sauce on the carpet, tons of broken toys, a hole in the wall in the hallway, and a backed-up toilet. The Hubs had been on his feet all day, cooking and replenishing the buffet table. I had to be "on" all day, chatting up people and filtering myself when someone said something kind of racist like, "I've never had oriental food before. Will there be cat?"

"I'm getting kind of tired of throwing this party," the Hubs said. "It's really a lot of work."

"Yeah, it was great the first couple of years when we only had twenty or thirty people."

"I mean, it's great that the business is growing, and it's awesome that so many people want to come, but today kind of sucked."

"I agree. I felt like all I did today was yell at other people's kids."

"Really? Like who?"

"The McCallister kids were jumping on our bed, the Dempsey twins drew on Adolpha's wall, and I had to tell the Cash kid's mom that he hit me across the face with a Nerf sword."

"Why were the Nerf swords out? I thought you locked up all that kind of stuff in the guest room."

I'd learned my lesson a few years before when a wilding pack of boys attacked guests with swords and guns. After that I designated one guest room as the off-limits space. That's where I locked up anything that could be used as a weapon. "The little bastard picked the lock."

"Wow. I think the party has gotten too big."

"Yeah, we need to cut back."

"But how? How do we decide who can come and who can't?"

"Maybe we can send out an email and let people know that we're cutting back on the invite list."

"What excuse can we give for cutting back?"

"I don't know. We could just be honest: the party is too big and we need to pare it down. It's not us, it's you."

"So we just tell them straight up: you can't come because you spilled soy sauce on the floor?"

"Exactly," I said. I grabbed a piece of paper and a pen and I started writing. "Okay, here is why you're not invited to our annual Chinese New Year party this year."

1. You've never deemed us worthy enough to join us in the past, so why waste another Evite on you?
2. You've attended in the past, but you barely speak to us while standing in our home and shoveling our food down your gullet.
3. You backed your car into another attendee's car and didn't tell anyone until we called the cops.
4. Your mom, your best friend, and your neighbor all bought new houses this year and you didn't call us.
5. You are not someone we'd be friends with on a normal basis and you're probably never going to move again, so step away from my egg rolls and let's just drop the act.
6. You didn't bring a hostess gift in the past. Would a plant I could kill later or a box of chocolates be too much to ask?
7. You brought a shitty hostess gift in the past. We're not Japanese, so please stop giving us sake.
8. You drink too much. What the hell? Our party is in the middle of the day; there is no need to get soused on the sake you brought us as a hostess gift.
9. You spilled soy sauce on our white rug—and our duvet. Yeah, our duvet. Which one of you animals ate food in my bed?

10. You want to sleep with my husband. You know who you are. I see how you flip your hair and laugh loudly at everything he says. He's not that funny, nor is he that interesting. Also, he's sort of dimwitted because he has no idea you're flirting with him.

11. You say racist things. Here's my PSA: "oriental" describes objects, as in "an oriental vase," while "Asian" describes people and culture, as in "Your daughter has beautiful Asian features."

12. Your kid(s) jumped on my bed, wrote on my wall, broke my son's favorite toy, taught my daughter how to "massage" her vagina, kicked a hole in my wall, hit me, hit my kids, hit my mother, used my lip gloss on her bunghole, ran through my screen door, took a dump behind the potted plant in the living room, and/or threw a fit when we didn't serve birthday cake or give out goody bags.

In case you're wondering, I never sent out this email. Instead, I took the scaredy-cat route and just never hosted another Chinese New Year party again. I've noticed that in the few years since I quit doing the party, my business has dropped off. I've decided to start throwing parties again, but it'll be a little different this time. I've rented the clubhouse at the park, and I'm taking guitar and hair-braiding lessons so I can lead the song circle when we sing "Kumbaya" at my first annual Earth Day party.

NICE HALLOWEEN COSTUME.
WAS SKANK SOLD OUT?

I belong to a local moms' group. They have playgroups and an online forum where there's always someone around at three A.M. to answer urgent questions about a clogged milk duct or to offer a recommendation for a great hairstylist. I like these things about the group, but if I'm being honest, I renew my membership every year because they plan silly fun stuff like random ladies' nights out at the gun range and a monthly happy hour. Every Halloween, they host a party for the entire family. Normally, it's a family-friendly event with face painting, a cake walk, and a photo booth. No alcohol, though; the only spirits offered are toddlers dressed in sheets.

Our family has attended the Halloween party every year. When Gomer and Adolpha were very small I would take them dressed up in coordinating costumes. We'd drag the Hubs along as well. The Hubs and I have never been big on dressing up in costumes. The closest thing that the Hubs has to a costume is a dumb T-shirt that says THIS IS MY COSTUME. I loved dressing up when I was a kid, but my costume was always something that I scavenged from my mom's closet. Because of my unlimited access to peasant skirts and scarves, I was always a fortune-teller or a witch. As an adult, I can never find a costume that I like. Most women's costumes are completely inappropriate. There's been an annoying trend I've seen crop up over the last several years. Can we talk about this for a second? I'm so perturbed about the sexy Halloween costumes that are taking over the aisles of Target and Walmart. What is the deal there? First it was sexy costumes for toddlers, which really pissed me off, because who thinks a sexy devil costume should come in 4T? Then the manufacturers branched out to try to capture the moms of these sexy little devils. I realize this isn't new—I remember the occasional sexy nurse or French maid costume from my childhood. But that's about it. It seems like over the years more and more normal costumes have been re-created as "sexy." I don't know when it became a thing for women to walk into a party dressed as a sexy vampire or a sexy dog. (Yeah, that costume exists. Imagine a brown spandex monokini with a tail and paw prints on the boobs. I don't know why there are paw prints on the boobs. I guess it's because that's the only way you'll know she's a dog and not some hot chick in a brown spandex monokini.) I guess I can kind of see the appeal of a sexy vampire, but I draw the line at a sexy piece of bubble gum. And why is it only the women? Where are the sexy costumes for the boys? How about a sexy Lego for Gomer or a sexy abominable snowman for the Hubs?

Thankfully, this sexy costume thing is a trend that most of my friends have avoided. Normally the mothers at this Halloween party dress all in black, pin a tail to their butt, throw some ears on a headband, and call themselves a cat. Or if they're really lazy they plop a pointy black hat on their head and declare themselves a witch. (I'm almost always a witch. I know, I know. Big surprise there.) The dads might occasionally bust out the Superman costume, but mostly so we can all laugh at their fake muscles.

Every now and again, the moms veer out of the costume comfort zone of cats and witches and try something a little different. You might see a Super Mom decked out in bright tights or a mom dressed as a clown in a wig and full makeup, but I've never seen anything too wild. At least, not until the year we saw the costume that prompted eight-year-old Gomer and me to have a discussion about male and female anatomy and how they fit together so nicely.

We'd just arrived at the party and I was trying to get my ghoulish-looking cupcakes over to the cake walk section. They were supposed to look like Frankenstein heads, but instead they looked like nuclear waste with bulging eyeballs. Either way, scary. Gomer went with six-year-old Adolpha and made a bee-line for the face painting. They were both pirates that year and they wanted some scurvy scars to go with their eye patches.

I finally deposited my sludgy-looking cupcakes and found a table to claim for our family. I dumped the Hubs and his smartphone in a seat and went off to socialize with my friends while he told everyone on Facebook how bored he was. A group of witches and cats were gathered by the drinks table, deep in discussion. I could tell something was afoot. Lots of scandalized looks were being thrown around and the eye rolls were out in full force. I love a good drama, so I decided to go there first and see what the hubbub was about.

". . . can't believe it," I heard one witch say as I approached the group.

"Thank goodness my kids are too little to get it," a cat said.

I poured myself some punch and asked, "What's going on?"

"Oh, hi, Jen," Sandi said, adjusting her cat ears, which were slipping off her head. "I didn't see you come in. Cute costume. Are you a cat, too?"

"I'm a dog, actually," I replied, shaking my head. "See? My ears are floppy, and no whiskers."

"Oh sure, I see it now. Love it."

"Thanks."

"Sometimes I wonder what people are thinking!" the lone clown in the group exclaimed. Her red cheeks got redder with anger.

"What happened, Sandi? What did I miss?" I asked.

"It's Marge. I guess you haven't seen her yet?" Sandi replied.

I shook my head. I didn't know Marge well. We didn't run in the same circles. She was part of the Mature Moms subgroup. They were the mothers of middle-school- and high-school-aged children and they didn't belong to playgroups anymore. They did weekly dinners together and took weekend antiquing trips—the kind of stuff we mothers of young children could only dream about.

"I haven't seen her tonight," I said, scanning the room for Marge. "What's she wearing?" Even though Marge was older than many of us, she was way hotter than all of us. Marge was a yoga instructor and her body was banging. She never hesitated to show it off any chance she could get. Every time she'd drop by our monthly happy hours, she was dressed in skintight pants and a sports bra. She would complain she was too warm to cover up, because she'd just finished teaching (or taking) a hot yoga class. She would drink white wine and tell us how bad the bowl of chips in the middle of the table was for our skin. We would tug at our frumpy sweatshirts and shamefully shove more chips in our mouths.

I had no idea what Marge was wearing that night, but I figured she was running around in a full-body catsuit or something. "Is she a sexy cat or something?" I asked.

"Worse. Wait until you see her," Sandi sighed. "Desmond hasn't figured it out yet, but he will soon enough. He's so bright for a four-year-old!"

"Just be glad you don't have a twelve-year-old," said a mom in a bathrobe and a shower cap, motioning toward a group of middle school boys giggling in a corner. "Can you imagine trying to explain that to them?" I nodded. I still had no idea what she was talking about, but I was too busy to care. I was making a mental note of her genius costume for next year. I wouldn't even have to do my hair.

Just then Marge came by carrying a stack of take-out pizzas. "Hi, girls!" Marge called as she breezed by. "Happy Halloween!"

She went by so fast that I didn't see her costume that well. From what I could tell, it didn't look like Marge's costume was sexy at all. It looked quite bulky, actually. I watched her drop the pizzas on the buffet table, but I still couldn't figure out what she was. She was wearing a black catsuit (figures), but it was covered by a huge off-white rectangular box that went to her knees, with her head sticking out the top and her arms out holes in the sides. It wasn't low cut enough to show off her bouncing beauties or high enough to show off her gorgeous gams. I was confused. What was everyone having a kitten about? "I don't get it," I said to Sandi.

"You will," she said.

I watched as Marge turned around to greet someone else. Now I could see the front of her costume, and I could clearly see that she was a standard electrical outlet.

"She's an electrical outlet?" I wondered. "That's weird. What's so bad about that?"

"Wait for it," Sandi promised.

"Hey, babe, can you bring me some more pizza?" It was Marge's husband, Art, calling to her from across the room.

"There," Sandi said.

I turned to see Art. He was also in a skintight black bodysuit (he was a weight lifter, so he looked good, too, of course) with a thick off-white cord rolling over his shoulder and down his chest toward his waist, where it ended in a giant three-pronged plug jutting out from his crotch.

"Are you fucking kidding me?" I asked Sandi. "He's a plug and she's the socket?"

Sandi nodded. "Yup. Now you understand why everyone is a little excited. Who does that at a party for kids?"

"I'm going to barf," I said. "Who wants to think about him putting his plug in her socket?"

"I think about him a lot," said a nearby cat. "And now I will even more. Did you see his ass in that costume?"

A witch giggled. "No, I was too busy admiring the size of his . . ."

"Amperage?" I teased.

"So you noticed it, too, Jen," the witch said, winking at me.

"How can you not? The first joke he makes about it being 'life-sized,' I will seriously lose my shit on him," I fumed. "What an asshole."

"Well, I think it's disgusting," the bathrobe lady said.

"Agreed," a cat said. "She could have been a sexy cat and no one would have cared."

"Or noticed," said Sandi. "I think that's the problem. They're attention whores."

About that time Gomer came looking for some food. "I'm hungry, Mom," he said.

"Okay," I answered. "Let's get you some pizza." We headed to the pizza table, where Marge was dishing out slices to everyone.

"Hi, Jen!" she said. "*Looove* your little pirate here. He looks adorable."

"Thanks, Marge."

"Are you a cat?"

"No, I'm a dog."

"You sure are!" Maybe I was a little sensitive, but I felt like her answer had nothing to do with my costume. "Pizza?"

"None for me. Just Gomer, please."

"Good choice. Pizza is terrible for your skin."

"Uh-huh."

"I'm surprised you haven't said anything about my costume," Marge said. "I know it's been all the talk tonight. It's a joke costume. People need to lighten up."

I didn't know what to say. Should I tell her that she was the scandal of the night? Should I tell her that people thought she and her husband were tacky attention whores? I love a good laugh, and I'm usually the last person in a room to have a sandy vagina and get offended easily by anything off-color, but come on! This was a family-friendly party with tons of inquisitive little kids who were at various stages of learning about the birds and the bees. Know your audience! You didn't see me grabbing the microphone from the teenager in charge of the cake walk and doing a two-minute riff about assholes in Congress and dropping *f*-bombs on the crowd. These costumes would have been terrific at an adults-only party. I would have laughed my ass off and probably posted their picture on Instagram. But when I'm around my kids and other people's kids, I am motherfucking Pollyanna. Even though I was thinking all of this, I didn't want to get into it with Marge. So I lied.

"I didn't even notice it. What are you?"

"I'm a socket. Art's the plug. Do you get it?"

"Yup. I get it."

So did Gomer. He looked around and saw Art yukking it up in the corner with some of the other miserable dads. I watched his eyes follow the thick cord over Art's shoulder and down to his man zone. Gomer looked at Marge and her strategically placed openings.

"Mom," Gomer said, "his plug fits in her socket?"

"It's hilarious," Marge said.

"Why is that funny?" Gomer asked.

"Um . . ." I said, stalling. I knew the moms of the twelve-year-old boys thought this was a tough conversation, but it wasn't very easy with an eight-year-old, either.

"Oh!" Gomer said. "I get it. The plug is where his penis goes and the socket is near her vagina. Is that why it's funny?"

I didn't know what to say, so I went with, "Guess so, Gomer."

I looked to Marge for help, but she just looked disgusted.

"Why did they make that their costume, Mom?" Gomer asked.

"That's a good question, Gomer. We should probably talk about it at home." I glared at Marge. "Go eat your pizza."

Marge watched him walk away and then whispered, "I can't believe that your child knows the words *penis* and *vagina*."

"Of course he does. He's eight. He can't call it a *pee-pee* or a *dingleberry* anymore."

"Fine. But he also knows about *s-e-x*?" She spelled the word. I couldn't believe that a woman standing there wearing a sexually provocative costume would spell the word *sex* like my grandmother would in church.

"Yes, he knows the basics, and now, thanks to your costume, he has a visual aid as well."

"What other things do you tell him? There's no reason for them to know anything. I would never teach my kids that kind of stuff when they're so young. Only perverts tell little kids about sex. What is wrong with you?"

She scurried away from me as if my bad parenting choices were the problem. She grabbed Art's (muscular) arm and whispered furiously into his ear while gesturing wildly at me. We made eye contact. He looked me up and down, taking in every inch of my sad dog costume. I could only guess what Marge had told him.

Gomer came up to me. "I know why they did it, Mom."

"What, Gomer?"

"The costume. It's a costume about sex. They can have sex in their costume. That's why it's funny." Gomer smiled, proud of himself. "You and Dad never dress up. Maybe you guys can do that next year."

I grabbed a piece of pizza (fuck my skin) and shoved it in my mouth so I wouldn't have to answer.

THANKSGIVING DAY PARADES SUCK WHEN THEY'RE NOT IN HD

Ever since Gomer was a baby, we've hosted Thanksgiving at our house. I'm not one to throw big parties (unless it's so I can drum up some business, as previously noted); I just figured it was easier to do it at my home. If everyone came to me, I didn't have to haul a Pack 'n Play, a bouncy seat, a Baby Bjorn, diapers, wipes, a change of clothes (for the baby and for me), a breast pump, bottles, a bottle warmer, and sixty other things that I carted around when I had a baby but can no longer remember because having babies kills brain cells.

I could see my extended family, eat some pie, and put my baby down for a nap all at the same time. That first year everyone felt bad for me, with all the work a newborn entails, so they brought all the food. I didn't argue with them, and that idea sort of stuck, so now I only have to clean my house and set tables for twenty to twenty-five people (we never know who might show up) and heat up some dinner rolls. The rest is taken care of by the family.

The Hubs does not get involved in the cooking or the baking required to put everyone into a food coma. Instead he busies himself with the entertainment side of things—namely, making sure that our televisions are optimized for the best viewing experience possible for parades, football games, and Lifetime and Disney movies.

We have enough places in our house for like-minded groups to spread out and watch what they want, but not all the TVs are created equal. In the past, the Hubs camped out in his movie room in the basement, claiming the best TV, but over the years, the kids have taken over his spot. He wasn't very happy when his favorite TV was playing *Mary Poppins* on a continuous loop. "This year we need new televisions before Thanksgiving," he announced.

"Why do we need new TVs?" I asked.

"The one in our bedroom and the one in the family room both need to go."

"Those two work just fine and we paid over a thousand dollars for each of them!"

"Yes, they turn on and off, the channels change, and the volume can go up and down, but they still aren't good. They're twelve years old and they're basically obsolete."

"Obsolete? How can they be obsolete? I don't even understand how that can be. We paid a fortune for them."

"They're enormous tube TVs. We can't watch anything in high-def, and they can't hook up to Netflix. They're ancient. They've got to go."

The one in the bedroom was sitting in an armoire that was starting to sag and buckle under the weight of the huge television. I had to admit it would be nice to not have the furniture break. But I still wasn't convinced.

"I don't know. It seems so wasteful. They're both in good shape."

"No. they both have to go. Your uncle Ralph hates watching the football game in the family room on that television, and if we got a better TV in our bedroom, we could send the kids there to watch their crap, and that would free up the projector in the theater for whatever inappropriate non–kid-friendly movie I want to watch, and you ladies would have a nice TV in the kitchen for Lifetime or whatever you watch. Jen, trust me, they're both dinosaurs and they need to be replaced. Don't worry. I'll take care of it," the Hubs assured me.

Over the next few days he researched new televisions. He also researched disposing of the two obsolete ones. What we found was astounding. First of all, the television that was breaking my armoire weighed in at one hundred and fifty pounds and the monster in the family room was a whopping three hundred pounds. Holy crap! What were we going to do with these things? We originally thought we'd sell them on Craigslist, because even though the Hubs found them to be outdated, I was sure that someone would find these televisions to be quite a nice addition to their homes. I placed ads the week before Thanksgiving, assuming that they'd be gone in an hour. Did I mention I paid a thousand dollars apiece for these things? I wrote what I thought was a compelling ad and only asked for twenty-five dollars and for the new owner to haul it away. The hell I was going to lug over a hundred pounds for a measly twenty-five dollars!

I posted my ad and waited patiently for my phone to ring. After twenty-four hours without a single call, I lowered my price to twenty dollars. Thanksgiving day was getting closer and I needed to get rid of these televisions. The Hubs had already ordered new TVs and they were due to be delivered any day now.

After three days without a nibble on my televisions, we started to look into other options. "We could donate them," I suggested.

"We can only donate the little one," the Hubs said. He meant the hundred-and-fifty-pound one in our bedroom. "The other one is too big and the donation center won't take it."

"How do you know?" I asked.

"I already called them."

"What will we do with the big one?" I asked.

"I don't know yet. I'm working on it."

"I don't want it to end up in a landfill," I reminded him.

"Don't worry. It won't. We can't dump it in the landfill. It's illegal. We have to have the television recycled."

"Oh. Well, maybe we should get the recycling company to come and get it, then."

"I don't want to do that yet," he said.

"Why not?" I asked.

"Because they charge you a hundred and fifty dollars to take it, and I don't think I should pay to recycle it. I'm doing the right thing here by not throwing it away; I shouldn't have to pay someone to recycle it."

"Can we offer it for free on Craigslist?"

"I've been trying. I've had it listed for free for weeks and not one call."

"For weeks? We just decided a few days ago to do this," I said.

"I hoped to have it all taken care of before we even talked about it. I didn't want to worry you. Unfortunately, we waited too long. These things are antiquated. No one wants them."

I dropped my Craigslist ad to free as well. I figured mine would get more attention than the one the Hubs placed. After all, I'm a "professional" writer. It's kind of my thing. To emphasize exactly how free these televisions were now, I capitalized the entire ad and yelled at everyone on Craigslist.

The Hubs brought his laptop over to me. "Look at how many

people are trying to get rid of the same televisions we are. It's time. We need to donate them."

"Donate them? Where? You said only one can be donated."

"That's true. Only this organization will take the little one." He showed me a website on his laptop.

I shook my head. "No way. I don't like that organization and what they stand for. I don't want to donate to them," I said.

"Why? What's wrong with them?"

"You know why I don't like them. They're one of those groups that think you can pray the gay away. I refuse to have their programs benefiting from my television."

The doorbell rang. It was the UPS man with the first new television.

The Hubs carried the box effortlessly into our bedroom. "Bedroom TV is here," he announced.

"Well, I don't know where you're going to put it, because I won't donate this one," I said, crossing my arms and scowling.

"Really? Now is when you're going to get super political on me? You ate at Chick-fil-A last week and I saw the bags in the car from Hobby Lobby," the Hubs said. "You just want to fight with me. Let me just show you what we've been missing." He proceeded to unpack the box and hook up the new television's bells and whistles. He viewed my YouTube channel and scrolled through a friend's Instagram feed. He called up *Orange Is the New Black* on Netflix and made me a soft nest in our bed. "You go ahead and watch this for a little bit while I get you a drink."

It didn't take me ten minutes to give up all my convictions. Damn you, Netflix! "Fine. We'll donate the little one. In the end I probably won't be funding anything they do, because it's very clear that no one wants these piece-of-shit televisions."

"I love you," the Hubs said. To the television.

"What about the big one?" I asked.

"Don't worry. I have that under control, too," he said. "Let's just focus on this one first. We need to get it out of the cabinet and into the minivan."

"I think we should hire someone," I said. "I can barely lift a fork to my mouth and you throw out your back every time you play Fruit Ninja on the Kinect. We'll drop it."

"No, Jen! The whole reason we're donating it is so that we don't have to spend any money. Hiring movers will defeat what we're doing here. You can do it. What do I always tell you? You're strong like what?"

"Strong like a bull," I said sulkily.

"That's right, my little bull. Now do some stretches, because we're going to get that bitch out of there."

It took us close to twenty minutes, but we manhandled that thing to the floor with me yelling "I don't have it! I don't have it!" the entire time. We were both slightly dazed and covered in a fine sheen of sweat. We looked at the television at our feet. "Okay," the Hubs said. "Now we just need to carry it out to the van."

"Are you kidding me?" I panted. "There is no way I can make it that far. That thing is a beast. It's heavy as shit and I don't have the wingspan to wrap my arms around it for a good grip. Please, let's call someone."

"I have a better idea," the Hubs said, darting from the room.

I looked at the massive television sitting in the middle of my bedroom and wondered if I could get used to it being there for the rest of my life, because there was no way in hell I was going to be able to muscle that thing to the garage. *I suppose it would make a nice bench to sit on when I'm putting on my shoes,* I thought.

The Hubs returned with our dolly. "We can put it on here and wheel it out the back door," he said. "The deck has the fewest stairs."

"That dolly is only rated to carry one hundred pounds. We're going to break it," I said.

"Nah, they always say that, but it can handle double that. It will be fine. Lift your end."

I screamed in agony as I tried to lift my half of the television onto the dolly. The rubber wheels groaned in protest. "It's too heavy!"

"It will be fine. Get the door." The Hubs tipped the dolly toward him and the television slid precariously. "Shit. A little help, Jen! You can't just walk away like that."

"I'm getting the door!" I yelled at him. "I can't hold the damn TV and get the door!"

"Fine. Just hurry," he panted, struggling under the weight of the dolly and the one-hundred-and-fifty-pound television.

"How much did that dolly cost?" I asked as I opened the door.

"I don't know. A hundred bucks, maybe. Why?"

"Just wondering. Because when you break it, you'll need to add that to your budget of 'money saved' by not calling anyone to haul this piece of shit away."

"No, that's not true. First of all, the dolly isn't going to break, and even if it did, it wouldn't count, because it's four years old and we've gotten a lot of use out of it. You've got to count depreciation."

"I just count replacement value."

The door to the deck was open, but it didn't look good to me.

The television was clearly wider than the doorway. "Help me, Jen," the Hubs said.

"I don't think it will fit through the door."

"It will," he said, shoving the dolly closer to the door jamb. "We just have to force it. I'll step out and pull. You stay in and push."

We assumed our positions and I crouched down to better push my end of the monstrosity through the doorway. "Push!" he yelled, grabbing the dolly and heaving it.

I heard the distinct sound of wood cracking. "Push harder!" he screamed. The sound got louder. I could see the wood trim around my doorway starting to splinter and buckle.

"Stop!" I shrieked. "The woodwork! You're destroying the trim!"

"It's okay," he replied. "I've got a guy who can fix that, no problem."

At that point I stepped back. "What the fuck are you doing?" I asked.

He stood up and faced me over the three-foot-tall television. "What?"

"This has become absolutely ridiculous. You refuse to spend a couple hundred dollars to have anyone remove this fucking television from our house, yet you are willing to sacrifice our dolly and our woodwork. Somehow those expenses don't matter to you. This has become personal with you."

"I told you. It's the principle. I shouldn't get charged to do the right thing. I'm not hauling this thing to a field and pushing it out of the back end of my car—"

"Assuming you could physically do that," I interjected.

"Right. I'm just saying, I could drop this thing in a ditch and let it rot and leach poison into the ground, but I'm not doing that. I'm trying to responsibly dispose of this thing, and every place I call wants hundreds of dollars from me. It's not fair!"

"But we didn't even need to do this," I reminded him. "*You* wanted new televisions."

"For your family! Thanksgiving is in a few days and your uncle will want—"

"This is not about my uncle. This is about you. You're pissed that the kids took over your man cave in the basement. I've always said we should do holidays the way we did when I was a kid. We never watched movies or television on holidays."

The Hubs rolled his eyes. "No. You guys played epic games of Uno and Risk."

"It was fun."

"It sounds like a nightmare. Especially when you refuse to play Stacking Uno."

"Stacking Uno? Is that the one where you can just continue to put down Draw Four cards until some sad sack is left with twenty cards?"

"Yeah, that one is fun!"

"Don't you remember? We tried that once. Adolpha cried the whole time and her hands were too small to hold all the cards you kept loading on her."

"She has two hands. I don't see the problem. Anyway, I'm not playing Risk with your family. I want to spend my Thanksgiving watching an R-rated movie on a new TV while my kids watch Disney somewhere else. Now, push!"

The woodwork groaned but held and the dolly banged onto the deck, dumping the television.

"Son of a bitch!" the Hubs growled. "Come on, Jen. Put your back into it, we're almost done."

We wrestled the television back onto the dolly and rolled it across the deck. "Watch out," the Hubs said. "I can do the steps on my own. I'm just going to bounce it down."

"Do you think that's a good idea?" I asked.

The Hubs pushed the dolly off the edge of the top step. One rubber tire popped.

"Sometimes I really hate you and how cheap you are," I said.

"I know, but we can't stop now. Go around and open the garage door and the back end of the van. I can do this." His face was turning red from the exertion and he looked like he might have a heart attack at any moment. But I really didn't care. I was furious with him. If he had a heart attack, I'd tell the EMTs to take the television with them in the ambulance, because I wasn't going.

I ran around the house, opened all the doors, and sat on the bumper to wait for him. No way was I going to go back and try to help him with his one-wheeled dolly. Fuck him. This was all his fault. And besides, I still had work to do to get ready for Thanksgiving and he was never going to help me. I always get ready by myself. He had one damn job and he couldn't even do it right!

I was sitting there seething when he finally dragged his load around the corner of the house. "Okay, Jen," he said, wiping his brow. "We just need to lift this up onto the bumper of the car and then slide it in."

"And wreck the paint job on my car? Hell no."

"Well, what do you suggest?"

I got a blanket and spread it out to protect my baby. "There. That should help."

We counted to three and heaved the television off the ground and into the car. I'm pretty sure a blood vessel burst in my eye.

"Okay, now we just need to take it to the donation center," the Hubs said. "Get the kids."

"You get the kids," I said, throwing myself into the passenger seat.

As the Hubs drove like a maniac to the center, the television slid precariously around the back end. "Could you stop taking turns so fast?" I asked.

"It's fine," the Hubs snapped at me. "Hey, Gomer? Do me a favor, buddy. Go ahead and unbuckle and turn around and hang on to that TV, would ya? If it hits the back door hard enough, it's going to break through and hit the car behind us."

"Are you fucking kidding me?" I whispered to the Hubs.

"Well, the hatch isn't that strong. It could happen. Don't worry, Gomer's got a strong grip on it now."

"Gomer! Sit down and buckle up. You do not need to hang on to that television. Your father just needs to drive slower and more carefully!"

"Relax!" the Hubs said. "Look, we're here." He pulled into the parking lot at the donation center. "Now, you run in and pretend like you're all alone and you need some help with a television. Just say that your husband is working today and couldn't help you."

"Are you serious?"

"Yeah. If I go in there and ask for help, they're going to think I'm a total pussy. Men shouldn't ask for help lifting stuff."

"You asked me to help you."

"That was different. You already know that I can't lift heavy stuff. Go on, go ask for help."

I went into the center and looked around. There were a few employees sorting and tagging items. They were all elderly women. Fuck. I approached the closest one. "Hi, um, yeah, I have a large television that I would like to donate today. It's in my car and my husband and I could use some help getting it in the store. So . . ."

The woman looked up from her tagging. "Of course, dear. Thank you so much for your donation. If you pull around to the back of the building and ring the bell, someone will help you."

"Oh, okay. So, there are other . . . younger . . . stronger . . . people here?"

"Yes, Carlos is in the back. He can help you."

"Okay, great. Thanks."

Carlos. That sounded promising. Surely he could at least lift my half and I could just supervise him and the Hubs.

I hopped in the car. "Drive around to the back," I said. "Carlos will help you."

We pulled up to the back door. There was a long ramp leading up to the door. The Hubs looked at it and turned a little green. "I hope Carlos can carry his half," the Hubs said. "I didn't eat lunch, and that can make a difference, you know."

I ran up and rang the bell. The door opened and an enormous man filled the doorway. "Hi, um, Carlos?" He nodded. "We have a large TV in the trunk of the car and we need some help getting it out."

Carlos didn't say anything; he just walked past me and went to the open trunk of the van. The Hubs was rearranging the blanket under the television. "Hey, Carlos," the Hubs greeted him. "Yeah, so it's a bit of a beast. Do you have a dolly or straps maybe that we could use? I didn't eat lunch. . . ."

Carlos looked at the television and rocked up one corner, testing the weight. He nodded, squatted down, and took that shit on his shoulder. "I—I—I can help you," the Hubs stammered, sort of reaching toward Carlos. Carlos turned and walked up the ramp with the television on his shoulder like it weighed no more than a sack of potatoes.

Carlos returned a minute later with a receipt and a smile. "Thank you," he said, and returned to the building, leaving my entire family slack-jawed.

"Did you see that, Dad?" Gomer asked.

"Wow," said Adolpha. "You're really weak, Daddy."

"I told you!" the Hubs snapped. "I didn't have lunch."

MY FIRST AND LAST MOTHER'S DAY PRESENT

On my first Mother's Day, I had a six-month-old baby. I was a brand-new mom, and all I wanted was a little recognition. Was that too much to ask? I'd paid my dues: I'd carried a baby. I'd gone through a dramatic pre-term birth where I was forced to have emergency surgery and my baby ended up in the NICU. I spent countless hours on crying jags trying to breast-feed a baby who weighed less than my boob. I finally got him to eat, and then I went out in public smelling like spoiled milk and sporting crusty chunks of spit-up on my shoulder or in my hair at all times. (I've never been real concerned with my personal appearance, but believe it or not, I do try harder than this.) I had severe back problems because every time I left the house I carried a baby, a car seat, a giant diaper bag, a stroller, a Baby Bjorn, a breast pump, an insulated pouch to hold my liquid gold, and enough toys, books, and snacks to keep Gomer happy until we could get home again.

I was ready to be honored and pampered that May. When the Hubs saw the first of a bazillion commercials reminding him that the big day was coming, he shrugged and said, "I don't have to get you anything."

"Yes you do. I'm a mother now."

"But you're not my mother," he argued.

"Are you kidding me?"

"Nope. You're Gomer's mother. Gomer needs to get you a gift."

"Gomer is a baby! He can't go and buy me a gift. You have to do it for him."

"You just need to wait until he's bigger and then he'll get you something."

I couldn't believe what I was hearing. I realize that there are times that the Hubs is a bit of an ass, but this was stunning. "You're not my father, but I'll still go and get you a shitty tie or something in June," I said.

"That's up to you. I didn't ask you to do that. I don't need another tie."

"I can't believe you're going to ruin my first Mother's Day," I wailed.

"How am I going to ruin it?" he said. "If you want a gift, go and get yourself a gift. It's like you said—Gomer's too little. He won't know."

"Don't you understand that you have to teach Gomer, Hubs? You have to be the one to take him to the store and help him pick out a card for me."

"He's a baby!"

"It doesn't matter. You have to start at some point or else he'll never learn."

"Fiiiiiine," he sighed, "but not this year. He's too little to understand. It would be a waste."

"A waste? A waste of what? Your precious time? Money?"

He shrugged. "All of it. This is stupid. I had no idea you were such a consumer. Since when does this stuff even matter to you?"

"It's my first Mother's Day, you asshole." I pouted like a toddler. "It's my special day."

"Everything is your special day! Your birthday, Valentine's Day, Christmas, and now I have to add Mother's Day to the list?"

"You forgot our anniversary," I reminded him "That's a special day, too."

"You're being ridiculous, Jen. Mother's Day isn't a real holiday."

"It is! Especially this year. This is my first one. I'm finally a mother."

"It's not like you struggled to get pregnant or something," he complained. "You're not the only mother in the world. There are millions of mothers. Billions, even."

"I don't care!" I cried. "This is the first time *I'm* a mother! And you'd better get me something nice to show me how much you appreciate me."

"You're such a drama queen, Jen. Fine. We need to replace our broken Dustbuster. I'll get you one of those. I saw one on sale the other day. It was a closeout."

"I don't want a Dustbuster for Mother's Day! And especially not one on clearance!"

"How about a stepstool? I never realized how short you were until we moved into this house. You can't reach a thing. It's annoying how much you bug me to put stuff away in all the places you can't reach. I was thinking of telling you to make a list of what you need because I'll only reach things for you twice a day, but a stepstool would be a lot easier on the both of us."

"I don't want a stepstool!" I yelled. "What is wrong with you?"

We glared at each other. I couldn't believe we were fighting over my Mother's Day gift. Why was it so hard for him to understand? I tried a different approach. "What do you normally buy your own mother for Mother's Day?"

"I don't know. It changes every year. It depends on what she needs," he said.

"Okay, well, what did you buy her last year?" I asked.

"Underwear," he said without hesitating. "I ordered it online and had it shipped to her."

"Underwear? You bought your mother underwear on the Internet? For Mother's Day?"

"Yeah. She was complaining that the ones she had were getting holey and starting to fall apart."

"You bought your mom underwear?" I asked again. I was stunned. I am close to my mom and I've bought her several gifts over the years. I usually buy her electronics or scarves or Christmas decorations, but I've never bought her underwear—for any occasion.

I knew that the Hubs' family was really into practical gifts, but I didn't realize just how practical.

"Underwear?" I said again.

"Yes! That's what she asked for!" he exclaimed.

I thought about the Hubs sitting at his laptop, scrolling through pages and pages of cotton granny panties, reading the reviews and trying to find the perfect pair for his mother. How did he know what size to buy? How did he know what brand she liked? How did he know if she wanted high-waist or bikini brief? Surely he didn't buy her thongs, right? I thought about my mother-in-law. Nope, she's definitely a full-coverage kind of gal.

I couldn't imagine my son ever buying me underwear, but

more important, I couldn't imagine ever asking him to! The year before the Hubs bought his mother underwear, he'd bought her wool socks and the year before that was a case of ChapStick to combat her chronic dry lips. I suddenly felt sorry for the Hubs. No wonder he didn't have a clue what to buy me for Mother's Day. I realized I needed to give him some ideas.

I smiled sweetly and said, "I don't want a Dustbuster, a step-stool, or underwear for Mother's Day. I want a special card from Gomer that I can save. Something about it being my first Mother's Day. Surely Hallmark will have something like that. I want my gift to be something I wouldn't normally buy myself."

He sighed. "Okay, I can do the card, but I still don't understand what gift you want."

"How about a gift card to somewhere? Like the salon where I get my hair cut? I haven't had a decent haircut since Gomer's been born."

He looked at my six-inch roots and said, "But those appointments take so long. Who will watch the baby while you're gone?"

I gritted my teeth and tried to be pleasant. "You would, dear. He's fairly easy now. I could go in the afternoon during nap time."

"I don't know. I like your hair the way it is," he said. I ran my fingers through my tangled, dirty hair and a handful of it fell out.

"Okay, how about a massage? My back is killing me from hauling all that baby gear. I'd love a massage."

"Ugh." The Hubs shuddered. "I would never want someone to rub on my body like that. How can you stand that?"

"It doesn't bother me."

"Maybe I should give you a massage?" The Hubs waggled his eyebrows at me.

"Now see, *that* bothers me. It's so not the same thing," I said. "I want the kind that doesn't come with a happy ending."

"The happy ending is the best part," the Hubs said.

"Says you. You cannot make my Mother's Day gift sex. That's so uncool."

"This is hard!" the Hubs said.

"No it's not. Just think pampering," I said.

"Pampering?" he repeated.

"I've been so busy with the baby that I haven't really had any time to take care of myself. I'd love a gift that helps me do that."

"Pampering," he muttered. "Take care of yourself."

"Maybe a day to myself? I'd love some alone time."

Suddenly a big smile came across his face. "I got it!" he said. "This is perfect!"

When Mother's Day rolled around, I was presented with a flat, square box and a card. I opened the card. It was a beauty. I'll give the Hubs this—he has a hard time being romantic, but he can pick out cards that make me cry every single time. I wiped my tears away and gave him a big kiss. "Thank you," I whispered. "This was perfect."

"Wait until you open your present," he said, bobbing up and down with excitement.

I tore off the wrapping paper to reveal a box that held a scale.

Let me repeat that. He gave me a scale. For Mother's Day.

"A scale?" The room was turning red. I was furious.

"Not just any scale!" the Hubs crowed. "This is a digital scale. It will tell you your weight to the quarter pound, *and* your body fat percentage."

I'm sorry, I was wrong. He bought me a *digital* scale. For Mother's Day.

"A digital scale?" I asked again. I was furious, but the Hubs didn't notice.

"Yeah! You said you wanted something that pampers you and helps you take care of yourself and that you'd never buy. A scale can do that for you. And this one is top of the line—you never would have bought one this nice for yourself. All kinds of spas use this kind of scale. It's like having a spa in your own bathroom. Happy Mother's Day!"

No, no, no, no! I wanted to scream at the Hubs. *You can't give me a scale for Mother's Day. I didn't want a Dustbuster or a stepstool, but either of those would have been better than a scale!*

After that first year, I always bought myself my own Mother's Day gift. Because nothing says "Happy Mother's Day, heifer" like a digital top-of-the-fucking-line scale!

THE EASTER I BLEW GOMER'S MIND

It was the day before Easter when I got the text message from my friend Lavinia:

HE KNOWS! her message screamed in all caps.

I knew immediately what she was talking about. "He" could only be Lavinia's son, Clifford. Lavinia is a self-proclaimed overachiever, and she's proud of it. She's done everything she could to make her only child's upbringing magical and amazing, but now, after nine years, Clifford was on to her.

I replied: *How do you know? Are you sure he knows?*

Gomer was nine now, and just that past Christmas he had been questioning the veracity of a man traveling around the world in one night with tiny flying reindeer. We'd managed to divert Gomer with the old "If you don't believe, he won't come" speech. It worked at the time, but who knew how much longer we had? Gomer and Clifford were getting older, and soon they'd guess the secret. I figured Clifford must have questioned the idea of a six-foot-tall bunny crawling through his window, and that sent Lavinia into a tizzy. I was ready to calm her down and reassure her that Clifford was just testing the waters, and then she wrote:

HE FOUND THE EASTER BUNNY'S STASH.

The stash? What did she mean by that? I was confused by her statement. Lavinia sets a much higher magical bar than I do, and sometimes I have a hard time following along when she's talking about her holiday prepping.

Me: What do you mean he found the stash?
Lavinia: The stash! Everything. The baskets, the grass, the candy, and all of the toys I bought for his basket.
Me: Ohhhh. *That* stash. Yeah, that changes everything.
Lavinia: Have your kids ever found your stash?
Me: No. Mostly because I don't have a stash. I never hide the baskets. My kids know they sit in the pantry on the shelf and then tonight I'll put them out when the kids go to bed and the Easter Bunny fills them with candy—mostly leftover stuff. We've been giving the same big chocolate bunnies for the past three years now because I think they're too big to eat so I just keep recycling them. I buy a few little toys that I've got to dig out of the trunk of the car or the back of my closet if I can remember where I stuck them and some new jellybeans every year and that's about it.
Lavinia: Don't they notice the chocolate bunnies are the same?
Me: Probably. I don't know. Maybe not? They're not really that bright when it comes to this kind of stuff. I put the

bunnies in the cupboard and they don't ask about them again. They think the Easter Bunny shops at Target and that Target stocks the same chocolate bunnies year after year.

Lavinia: Well, Clifford is really sad and confused.

Me: What did you say to him when he found the stash?

Lavinia: Nothing. I just diverted his attention, but he saw his basket and the grass and all the toys for his basket. He asked me why they were in the closet. I told him that sometimes I store things for the Easter Bunny because he can't carry it all. Then Newman took him out for frozen yogurt so I could move it all to a new, more secure location. But it's too late. It's all ruined! He knows. I know he knows. He's figured it out. It's over!

At this point, I didn't know what to say. I like Lavinia a lot, but I couldn't relate. I'm not that big on the magic at my house. Sure, we do Santa and the Tooth Fairy and that sort of thing, but our magic is really lame compared to Lavinia's. I've never had our Elf on the Shelf bring gifts. I've never stenciled little green leprechaun footprints on the floor. I've never dropped a glitter bomb and twenty bucks for a first tooth. We're pretty basic around our house. My kids have fairly low expectations, so the idea of blowing my kids' idyllic childhood with a hidden stash of goodies wasn't anything I could understand.

I might not be an overachiever, but I'm pretty sneaky, so I had an idea that could save the day for at least another year.

Me: Get him something else. Something big. Like a bike or something. Something that *you've* always said no to, but the *Easter Bunny* says yes to. Something dangerous and/or expensive.

Lavinia: That's what Newman said, too! I think you're right. Clifford broke his DS earlier this year because he was careless with it and we told him he needed to save his money to buy a replacement. He'd be stunned if the Easter Bunny brought him a brand-new DS.

Me: There you go. That should work.

Lavinia: Let me think about it. Thanks for talking me down. I know it doesn't seem like a big deal to you, but it really bothered me.

Me: I understand. It's really important to you. But you know, the boys are nine now. They won't believe in this stuff much longer. We might as well get used to the idea now.

Lavinia: I know. But he's my only one. I've got to try to make it last as long as I can.

I put down my phone and thought about how I'd feel if Gomer stopped believing in Santa and the Easter Bunny and all of it. I decided it was no big thing. I'm not that Overachieving Mom who makes it spectacular and magical. I'm not that mom who totally gets excited watching my kids' eyes light up on Christmas morning when they see what Santa brought them. I couldn't care less. In fact, I told myself, I'd be relieved when it was all over and out in the open! I wouldn't have to hide my pile of goodies or stay up late on Christmas Eve to build toy kitchens and doll houses. I wouldn't have to wake up in a panic the morning after Adolpha lost a tooth and make up some lame story about the Tooth Fairy being afraid of the dark so she couldn't venture into Adolpha's room to leave her a dollar and instead she left the money on the kitchen counter. Frankly, I was exhausted from making up Tooth Fairy lies. That chick drove me nuts! No, I wouldn't be sad like Lavinia, because life would be so much easier when they knew. I'd be happy when they knew!

Later that night I was reading to my kids before bed when Gomer announced giddily, "Adolpha, I'm so excited, aren't you? I can hardly wait for the Easter Bunny tonight. I wonder what he'll bring us!"

Adolpha shrugged. "He doesn't bring much. He's not like Santa. He only brought me a book and a DVD last year. Even his candy isn't as good as Santa's. In fact, I think last year he gave me the chocolate bunny that Mom put in the cupboard from the year before."

"Hmm . . . I never thought about it. You might be right."

Uh-oh, I thought. *Adolpha might figure out this whole scheme before Gomer does!*

"Well, it doesn't matter! I'm still excited," Gomer exclaimed. He snuggled under his covers. "I'm going to go to sleep extra early tonight!"

Okay, he knows. He totally knows, I thought. At this point, I assumed Gomer was acting. There was no way this kid still believed that hard. I was sure he was putting on an act for his sister.

"I hope the Easter Bunny brings me a Halo guy," he said.

Crap. I had no idea what a "Halo guy" was. He was getting some cheap DVD out of the kid movie clearance bin at Walmart and a Lego set.

"What are you hoping for?" I asked Adolpha. Maybe I was correct in my thinking that she still liked stuffed animals. Getting it right for one out of two isn't so bad.

She shrugged again. "I dunno. Whatever. It'll be fine."

Good girl.

I went back to reading, and then Gomer interrupted me. "Hey, Mom! I've been thinking about something."

"What's up?"

"Are parents the Easter Bunny?"

I put down the book. "What do you think?" I asked.

"I don't know. That's why I'm asking."

"Okay," I said.

"Are you?" he asked.

"Well, you know, if you don't believe, he doesn't come," I said, turning back to my book, assuming the thought of possibly losing out on a Halo guy and some crappy chocolate would shut him up and our conversation would be over for another year.

He sighed heavily, exasperated. "I know that. It's just that I think . . . maybe . . . it's you."

"Hmm," I said, neither confirming nor denying.

"I just don't see how it can be done otherwise. There are so many kids in the world and just one Easter Bunny."

"He's magic, Gomer!" Adolpha said.

"I'm not sure I believe in magic anymore, Adolpha," Gomer said. "Tell me, Mom. Is it you?"

"Hmm," I said again, trying to buy some time while my brain worked on a fairly elaborate lie that involved wormholes for the Easter Bunny to travel through.

"Stop that!" Gomer said. "Just tell me the truth."

"The truth?"

"Yes," Gomer said. Then he looked me square in the eye and said, "And don't lie."

Oh no, I thought frantically, *shit just got real.* See, in our house we have a rule: if someone says "Don't lie," then you can't lie. No matter what. It's impossible. Not a white lie, not a gray area. Nothing. When Gomer asked me where babies came from when he was five, he used the "don't lie" move on me, and suddenly he became the most educated kid in kindergarten. "Don't lie" is a big deal around here.

"Don't lie?" I asked carefully, hoping he'd change his mind.

"Nope. The truth." He crossed his arms and stared me down.

"Adolpha, please go brush your teeth," I said.

"Whyyyyy?" whined Adolpha.

Because I'm going to blow your brother's mind and I need you to stay innocent for another year, kid, that's why!

"Because I said so."

She huffed out of the room and left me and Gomer alone.

"Are you sure you want to know?" I asked, closing his bedroom door.

"Yes," he whispered.

"Are you sure you can handle the truth?" I asked.

"Oh yeah," he said.

"Okay. Ask me your question again."

Gomer took a deep breath. "Are parents the Easter Bunny? Don't lie."

I waited half a second and then I nodded slightly.

What happened next was like something out of a cartoon. His eyes bugged out of his head, and if there was a sound effect, it would have been that *awoooga wooooga* noise. He fell over onto his side and lay there for a moment, perfectly still.

Holy shit. I really did *blow his mind!*

"Gomer?" I asked. "Are you okay?"

He sat back up. He wasn't crying, but his eyes were shiny and he looked like he might lose his shit at any moment.

"You really didn't know?" I asked incredulously. He shook his head. "You didn't suspect at all?" He shook his head again. *What sort of bubble did this kid live in?* I wondered.

"No," he sighed heavily.

I didn't know what else to say except "Oh."

I felt terrible. I had ruined what little magic I actually do. I should have lied! I should never have told him the truth! Now *I* was going to cry!

"You said 'don't lie,'" I said, trying to put the blame back on him. "You shouldn't have said that. You know how serious that is."

"I know," he said. He was quiet for a minute, and then he said, "Well, at least Santa is still real, right?"

The horrified expression on my face told him everything he needed to know.

His hopeful little face fell and he screeched, "He's you, too? *You* gave me the skateboard last year?"

I nodded. *God, I suck at parenting,* I thought. I was ruining everything for him, but I couldn't stop myself. It had been so hard living this lie for so long. It felt good to come clean and to tell him the truth.

"Of course you're Santa! Only a mom would give a helmet and knee pads and wrist guards along with the skateboard. Santa would never do that."

"I want you to have fun but still be safe," I said, gently stroking his head.

Gomer sat quietly for a few minutes thinking of all the gifts he'd received from "Santa" over the years. "The skateboard . . . the DS . . . all of those Legos. Hey, wait! You said I couldn't have the Lego Death Star because Santa's elves couldn't make it," he said accusingly. "You just didn't want to buy it!"

"Gomer, that is a four-hundred-dollar Lego set! There was no way I was going to buy that for you."

"Yeah," he sighed.

Adolpha stuck her head in the door. "What are you guys doing in here? Mommy, are you going to tuck me in?"

"Yes!" I yelled, panicking. "Get to bed!" I couldn't take the chance that Gomer would ruin the magic for Adolpha. "Go! I'll be there in a second."

Once Adolpha shut the door again, I turned to Gomer. "Listen, this is a big deal. You're a big boy now who knows a big secret. You *cannot* ruin it for the little kids around you. You can't tell Adolpha or anyone else what you know. Sherman knows, but Violet does not, and Uncle C.B. and Aunt Ida will be really irritated if you ruin it for her. If you ruin this for *any* little kids, you will be in huge trouble. Got it?"

Gomer solemnly nodded his head. "Got it," he said.

"Good boy," I said, kissing him. "You're part of the magic now."

I was worried Gomer would be sad the next day. However, he was anything but. I had warned him within an inch of his life not to spill the beans, and he really took my warning to heart. When he saw his Easter basket the next morning he overexaggerated for Adolpha's sake.

"Loooooook, Adolpha. The Easter Bunny came last night and brought us some great stuff from his house, not at all from Target!" he exclaimed, and winked at me.

Real subtle, Gomer.

When they went out to hunt for Easter eggs at my mom's house, Gomer was just a tad over the top. "Oh my! The Easter Bunny has been soooooo busy hiding all of these eggs, Adolpha. He's soooo magical and amazing!" He gave my mom a wink that time.

That night when I tucked him into bed I told him I was proud of him for keeping the secret and doing a great job being such a big boy now.

He said, "It's okay, Mom. I was sort of sad at first, but then I remembered I still have the Tooth Fairy and the Elf on the Shelf. Those aren't you, right?"

Suddenly I knew exactly how Lavinia had felt the night before. I wasn't ready. Sure, I don't love keeping all the magic alive, but I hate even more how fast Gomer is growing up. I might not love moving a doll around or pretending to find dollar bills on the counter, but I love keeping Gomer little for a bit longer.

I smiled and kissed him, "Of course not. Goodnight."

Hey, he didn't say "Don't lie."

Acknowledgments

Wow, acknowledgments are tough. What if I forget somebody? That's a lot of pressure. All right, let's try this. I'm going to do my best. If I forget you, I apologize profusely. It was an accident. Or maybe it wasn't. Who knows?

To my mom and dad: Thank you for always encouraging me to tell my stories. Thank you for giving me a childhood that we can *all* laugh at when we look back on it. Thank you for putting up your Christmas decorations in August.

To the Hubs: Thank you for always believing in me, even when I don't believe in myself. Thank you for encouraging me to write and supporting me while I write. Thank you for buying me front-loaders for Christmas (that totally makes up for the scale for Mother's Day). How about we get a new dishwasher this year? Thank you for being my best friend and making me laugh every day. Thank you for feeding our kids and for paying our bills on time.

To Gomer and Adolpha: Put this book down, you're too young to read it. Now go to bed. Mommy loves you.

To Robin O'Bryant: Thank you for your words of advice and

encouragement. Thank you for sharing your wisdom and your experience with me. I would like to be a sister wife—where do I apply?

To DG: Thank you for taking my frantic calls and for always knowing the right thing to say to me. Thank you for supporting everything I do and for being one of my biggest cheerleaders. And thank you for the mug. I drank hot cocoa from it in July when I was writing this book, just to get me in the proper mood.

To Nikki Knepper: Thank you for being the kindest and most loyal friend out there (who also sends me mugs—I guess I really like mugs). You are fearsome and soft and cuddly all at once, and you have the biggest heart of anyone I know. Don't worry, I won't tell anyone.

To my tribe: When the water rises all boats rise.

To Christie R.: Thank you for coming up with the idea for this book. I owe you lunch.

To the W family: Thank you for giving my lazy ass Choppy Elfie and thus starting this whole adventure.

To my readers: I am so excited and amazed that anyone cares what I have to say. I love every email, comment, and tweet you send me. Don't tell the Hubs, but *you* are the wind beneath my wings!

And last but not least, I want to acknowledge all the bloggers out there who are pouring their hearts and souls out every day for themselves and their readers. So many of us write because we have something to say. We have something we want to share with the world. It's an outlet and it's cathartic, but it's also a passion. We're all looking for an audience who can hear our voice and appreciate it. To those bloggers I want to say, don't stop writing. Your people are out there and they will find you, but they won't find you if you give up.

I'm the one on the right. My dad was obviously going for a "my two sons" look that year when he decided to dress us in matching Steve Austin track suits.

JEN MANN is the nationally bestselling author of *People I Want to Punch in the Throat,* based on her popular blog of the same name. She has also written for *The Huffington Post,* Scary Mommy, NickMom, Babble, Circle of Moms, and CNN Headline News. Her book was a finalist in the 2014 Goodreads Choice Awards and her blog received a 2014 Bloggie Award for Best Parenting Weblog. She lives in Overland Park, Kansas, and is married to "the Hubs" and is the mother of two children whom she calls Gomer and Adolpha on her blog. She swears their real names are actually worse.

peopleiwanttopunchinthethroat.com
Facebook.com/peopleiwanttopunchinthethroat
@Throat_Punch

ABOUT THE TYPE

This book was set in Minion, a 1990 Adobe Originals typeface by Robert Slimbach (b. 1956). Minion is inspired by classical, old-style typefaces of the late Renaissance, a period of elegant, beautiful, and highly readable type designs. Created primarily for text setting, Minion combines the aesthetic and functional qualities that make text type highly readable with the versatility of digital technology.